THE ECONOMIC IMPLICATIONS OF

ADVERTISING

THE ECONOMIC IMPLICATIONS OF

ADVERTISING

O. J. FIRESTONE

Commissioned by
THE INSTITUTE OF CANADIAN ADVERTISING

METHUEN

TORONTO & LONDON

1967

THE ECONOMIC IMPLICATIONS OF ADVERTISING

Published in Toronto by
Methuen Publications
(A Division of The Carswell Company Ltd.)
and in London by
Methuen & Co Ltd

Printed and bound in Canada by
The Carswell Printing Company

Foreword

The Government of Canada, concerned over a trend of rising prices, established in the autumn of 1966 a Special Joint Committee of the Senate and House of Commons on Consumer Credit (Prices) to study and report upon consumer credit and those influences in the economy that might be contributing to upward pressures on the cost of living in Canada.

Effective marketing, in an industrialized, mass production economy, is an essential component of operating efficiency. Since advertising, as a basic marketing tool, is an integral element in the modern production and distribution process, the Special Joint Committee desired to explore, among other things, the role of advertising and its possible effects upon prices.

At the Committee's invitation, therefore, the Institute of Canadian Advertising, the trade and professional organization representing the advertising agencies of Canada, presented a brief on "the role of advertising in the Canadian economy, the contribution it makes to economic growth and social welfare, its effects on consumer satisfaction and prices and related matters".

The Institute felt that it would be helpful to the investigations of the Special Joint Committee to have available also an

v

213773

independent, professional assessment of the role of advertising, prepared by a qualified economist. Accordingly, the Institute asked Professor O. J. Firestone, the Vice-Dean of the Faculty of Social Sciences of the University of Ottawa, to undertake an analysis of the economic implications of advertising. Professor Firestone is the author of several books in economics, the most recent being *Broadcast Advertising in Canada, Past and Future Growth*. Included as an exhibit to the I.C.A. brief, Dr. Firestone's study was submitted to the Special Joint Committee as a public service on December 13, 1966.

Dr. Firestone has produced a comprehensive review of the role and implications of advertising. The work here has particular reference to the Canadian economy, but its applications are international in scope and thus are far-reaching in their significance. Thoughtful, analytical and well documented, this study by a professional economist has already become one of the most important statements of an essential aspect of today's business.

Institute of Canadian Advertising

Toronto, Canada
February 1, 1967

Contents

Introduction

In the first session of the twenty-seventh Parliament of Canada (1966), the Special Joint Committee of the Senate-House of Commons on Consumer Credit (Prices) asked the Institute of Canadian Advertising to appear as witness and to present evidence on the subject of the economic implications of advertising.

The terms of reference of the Special Joint Committee of the Senate-House of Commons on Consumer Credit (Prices) were as follows:

> To enquire into and report upon the problems of consumer credit and report upon the trends in the cost of living in Canada and factors which may have contributed to changes in the cost of living in Canada in recent months.

Since advertising is one of the factors that may be contributing to rising costs and prices, the Special Joint Committee wished to avail itself of such information as could be obtained to throw light on the subject. The Institute of Canadian Advertising, representing the advertising agencies of Canada, undertook to present a brief to the Special Joint Committee and to appear as witness on the date designated by the Committee, December 13, 1966.

The Institute of Canadian Advertising felt that it might be helpful to the Special Joint Committee if, in addition to its submission, there was made available "an independent and authoritative professional analysis of the economic implications of advertising—with particular reference to the Canadian situation". The Institute asked the author to undertake such a study within the limitations of time available, and it suggested that the study should deal with such questions as:

> The effect of advertising on the Canadian economy, on business, the consumer, costs and prices, productivity, competition, employment, social welfare and economic growth generally.

The Institute of Canadian Advertising emphasized that it wished to make available to the Special Joint Committee an independently prepared economic study on advertising as a public service contribution. Thus this study represents solely results of research work and analysis which the author has done, some of which was published by the University of Ottawa Press earlier this year under the title *Broadcast Advertising in Canada, Past and Future Growth,* as well as some new work.

The difficulties in undertaking this study were in part time limitations. But even more limiting was the lack of adequate data relating to advertising and its effect on costs, prices, sales, profits, competition, scale of operations, consumer spending, communication media, and on economic activity in general. Nor were there available systematic surveys that would provide comparable data relating to the main economic effects over a period of time or on a basis comparable with other countries. Still further there exist in Canada very few studies dealing with quantitative and qualitative aspects of the impact of advertising on consumers, nor do there exist such studies dealing with the motivations of advertisers and the use of advertising either to enhance or to reduce competition.

Such statistical and economic investigations have been carried out increasingly in other countries, particularly in the United

States and in the United Kingdom. In the absence of such quantitative information and assessment in Canada, however, all that this study could attempt to do was to present a summary of some of the relevant literature on the subject of the economic implications of advertising, a brief review of available data, and a preliminary survey of the present situation and past developments, together with an indication of some of the problems faced in Canada.

The gaps in knowledge in the quantitative area are greater than the data available. This points to the urgency for a serious attempt to be undertaken at some systematic data gathering, analysis and research if decision makers in the legislature and in government—as well as in business—wish to base their decisions on knowledge of facts, evidence and assessment of implications, rather than on hearsay and unproven opinions. Indications of some of the major gaps that exist in the area of the role of advertising in the Canadian economy, its effect on employment, income, productivity, competition and prices, are mentioned throughout the study and listed in summary form in the appendix.

It is hoped that increasingly the advertising agencies, the major advertisers and the communication media will realize that it is in the best interest of all Canadians if more is known about the economic effects of advertising. Advertising has been maligned as well as praised as a major factor in the Canadian way of life. Little purpose is served by exaggerating in either direction.

What is needed is systematic, quantitative and qualitative research and analysis—carried on in an objective and independent way—which will throw light on a number of questions as they concern the effectiveness of advertising, its impact on consumers and the economy as a whole, and its relationship to the public interest.

The primary responsibility to initiate research work in the field of advertising rests with industry. But since the public interest is also involved, the requirements for systematic data collection and investigation, as well as research, should receive the sympathetic encouragement of Government.

This study is but a minor contribution to the subject of the economic implications of advertising. Its main objective is to stimulate discussion of some of the issues involved, based on whatever modest quantitative information is available. A corollary aim is to emphasize the importance of filling some of the gaps that exist in the knowledge of the role of advertising in the Canadian economy, so that in the future both constructive comments and adverse criticism will be based on facts rather than on conjecture.

*   *   *

The above introduction represents the text as contained in the study submitted to the Special Joint Committee of the Senate and House of Commons on Consumer Credit (Prices) on December 13, 1966. The Co-Chairman, Senator David A. Croll, described the study as "an excellent reference" which was "placed on the record" of the Committee.[1] The Co-Chairman further commended the Institute of Canadian Advertising for taking the initiative in having the author prepare this study which, according to Senator Croll, "will become a reference document of the first order because this is just the beginning of the public interest and the public discussion of this topic".[2]

A limited number of copies of the study were prepared for submission to the Special Joint Committee. These were all distributed on the first day of presentation of the document to the Committee. Demand for copies of this study came from many sources in Canada, the United States and from overseas, and this led Methuen Publications of Toronto to undertake the publication of the study in book form.

---

[1] *Proceedings* of the Special Joint Committee of the Senate and House of Commons on Consumer Credit (Prices), December 13, 1966, p. 1991.
[2] *Ibid.*, p. 2055.

This printed version of the study retains all the material and conclusions contained in the original document submitted to the Special Joint Committee. Two minor adaptations were made:

1. Some editorial changes were made, including the addition of some supplementary material which was not available when the study was completed.

2. New estimates for 1966 which had become available were incorporated.

This study would not have been undertaken but for the persistent and wise counsel offered by the President of the Institute of Canadian Advertising, Bryan Vaughan. John N. Milne, Vice-President in charge of research, MacLaren Advertising Company Limited, made a number of pertinent comments. To these two and the many other readers of the study who offered constructive suggestions go my sincere thanks. I am also very much indebted to the editors of Methuen Publications who saw the book through the press and to Mrs. L. Rowntree, who typed the manuscript and worked helpfully on the subject index.

O. J. FIRESTONE
Professor of Economics
University of Ottawa

Ottawa, Canada
February 1, 1967

1

Definition

Concept of Advertising

Advertising involves the communication of a message to the public, that message being designed to achieve an objective; the objective will vary, depending on whether the advertisement serves a business purpose or a public purpose.

Business objectives include the aim of a seller to advise a potential buyer of goods and services for sale, their quality, their usefulness, their effectiveness, their availability, their price, and all the other elements of information which may affect the buyer's decision to purchase the items advertised. The advertiser may be a business firm, or he may be an individual who uses a classified advertisement in a newspaper, to find a job or sell a used car, for instance.

Public objectives include advertisements placed by government authorities and public and private non-profit institutions which aim at informing the public about a given situation and persuading it to heed the message—for example, a public service advertisement designed to encourage safe driving.

To formulate and transmit an advertising message involves the purchase and use of space or time on one or several mass

1

communication media. Thus advertising represents a link between three elements in the social structure: (a) the communicator, i.e. the advertiser (businessmen, governments or institutions); (b) the recipient of the advertising message, i.e. the consumer or other sectors of the public; and (c) the media, i.e. the institutions and corporations, private and public, that control the instruments of mass communications. In the second half of the twentieth century, advertising, more than ever before, has become a means of mass communication for hire.   *P.1*

The bulk of advertising is directed toward facilitating the sales efforts of business. Since it is this type of advertising that has been exposed to the greatest criticism and is the subject of proposals for a tax to be imposed, this study concentrates on this particular part of advertising efforts in Canada.

When business firms address advertising to their potential customers, these may be either consumers (that is, the final users of goods and services produced), or they may be other businessmen, or government authorities or other public bodies. To reflect this difference in customers, the distinction is usually made between consumer advertising and industrial advertising. The bulk of advertising effort is made to influence consumers.

While the main concern of this study is consumer advertising, it should be borne in mind that whenever reference is made to the advertising industry and advertising expenditures, these cover all advertising efforts, whether they are addressed to the private sector of the economy, consumer and business firms, or to the public and semi-public sectors of the economy, including governments and institutions.

Content of Advertising

Some economists make the distinction between the "informative" content of an advertising message and the "persuasive" content.

The *informative* content brings to the attention of a potential buyer the type of the commodity or service for sale, its quality, serviceability, usefulness and price.

The *persuasive* content of an advertising message refers to that part of the advertisement that attempts to translate latent wants on the part of an individual into effective demand for a good or a service, encouraging the prospective customer to purchase the specific product or service advertised.

This differentiation between the "informative" and "persuasive" content of advertising is frequently made by those critics who are prepared to accede that "informative" advertising has a constructive and developmental role to play. But this, they claim, does not apply to the "persuasive" aspect of advertising, which may aim at the consumer buying goods he does not need, paying higher prices for that commodity than would be necessary in the absence of such advertising, and which may bring about a reduction of competition through excessive advertising creating market power, preventing or reducing new entries into industry, or generally strengthening monopoly or oligopoly situations.

In the latter type of situation, the consumer cannot evade the additional costs of advertising by turning to lower-priced unadvertised goods simply because monopolists and oligopolists will keep such commodities from coming to the market. Professor Harry G. Johnson explains:

> This possibility is realized when a monopolistic firm uses heavy advertising expenditure to maintain and expand its market, and much more commonly when the production of a commodity is concentrated in the hands of a few firms, who compete with each other by heavy advertising of trivially differentiated varieties of the product—what economists call oligopoly with product differentiation. Cigarettes, soap, and gasoline are typical examples. In these cases, advertising clearly involves economic inefficiency and an unnecessary waste of resources, and may contribute to the retardation of technical progress. In this context, advertising poses essentially the same problem for policy as the patent system—both are in principle devices for stimulating progress, which may in fact lend themselves to the support of monopoly and resistance to change. The fundamental problem in these cases, however, is not advertising as such but the oligopoly situation which the use of advertising reinforces, and the solution would seem to

rest with combines policy rather than intervention in advertising.[1]

The essence of the advertising message, whether "informative" or "persuasive", or both, is to give the consumer a choice in selecting, if he so wishes, one or another commodity. Thus advertising adds to the consumer's stock of knowledge.

Professor Lester G. Telser, of the University of Chicago, explains the relationship between advertising and the consumers' stock of knowledge in these terms:

> Consumers have initially a stock of knowledge about goods and services of which part comes via advertising messages and the rest through various channels including conversations with friends, experience with products, shopping trips, and discussions with salesmen. Not only does acquisition of knowledge about goods and services take time and trouble, it may also require money outlays. Moreover, the stock of knowledge about products becomes obsolete with the passage of time because terms of sale change, new products appear and old ones disappear or change, tastes alter, and there is forgetting. All these factors underlie the consumer demand for information about goods and services of which one source is advertising messages. . . .
>
> Essential to the maintenance of the stock of knowledge about goods is the identifiability of sellers and/or the branding of goods. Without these the knowledge gained in each instance could not be effectively used on subsequent occasions. Sellers must keep their identity and the identity of the goods they sell before the public so as to capture the benefit of good will from prior experience. . . . The effect of advertising on sales is partly due to the fact that advertising adds to the stock of knowledge about products and stimulates sales for a period of time following the transmission of advertising messages. . . .
>
> The demand for knowledge about products differs because of various circumstances. Thus if a commodity remains unchanged over a long period and has a steady clientele, it tends to be less promoted. Hence it is less advertised. Commodities which

---

[1] *The Canadian Quandary: Economic Problems and Policies*, by Harry G. Johnson, McGraw-Hill Company of Canada Limited, Toronto, 1963, p. 281.

do not satisfy these stability conditions, tend to be more promoted and more advertised.[2]

Few critics of advertising would deny the essentiality of adding to consumers' knowledge in modern society, or that in the present stage of social development, advertising by business is not a direct and economic means of achieving this objective. But the main points of the controversy are: What is essential and what is not? What is useful and what is not? What is wasteful and what is not? These questions are dealt with further in Chapters 2 and 3.

From the point of view of clarifying definitions, the question arises whether a split between the "informative" content and the "persuasive" content of advertising is of more than academic interest. And the related question is whether this distinction has much practical meaning for policy formulation.

On this point, the proponents of advertising appear to feel rather strongly:

> Advertising is selling. . . . The object of advertising is not basically to inform, but to inform for the purpose of selling. The information given will be that which is calculated to help the proposition. No one is going to pay large sums of money to give information which hinders his proposition. Often the amount of information is valid; sometimes it is minimal because there is no new information to give. Advertising neither is nor can be a disinterested service of consumer information. It is salesmanship on a mass scale.[3]

Professor Johnson describes the distinction between the "informative" and "persuasive" type of advertising as "extremely difficult to draw". He says further:

> On the one hand, the mere offering of objective information may itself be a persuasive act; . . . on the other hand, as

---

[2] "Supply and Demand for Advertising Messages", by Lester G. Telser, *American Economic Review*, May, 1966, pp. 462-464.

[3] "The Social and Economic Context of Advertising", by John Hobson, Lecture I of the Three Cantor Lectures dealing with *The Influence and Techniques of Modern Advertising*, The Royal Society for the Encouragement of Arts, Manufactures and Commerce, London, March 2, 1964, Reprint, p. 2.

society becomes wealthier, it becomes less and less true that people use goods solely for their objective qualities. The use of goods has social and personal connotations which people may quite legitimately wish to buy—the claim that fashionable people serve a certain kind of spaghetti to their guests may be information rather than persuasion, as any reader of women's magazines is well aware. The employment of persuasion by advertisers is, however, indisputable; and it raises broader issues than the question of waste.[4]

Another economist, Professor Walter Taplin, makes the point how inconsistent critics of the persuasive aspects of advertising are when they say: "Persuasion in politics is justified; in business it must be regarded with suspicion."[5] For, as Professor Taplin explains, persuasion is the normal method of influencing decisions in a democracy, and this applies to both politics and business as long as the "rules of the game" are followed. In the case of business behaviour, this refers to operating within the competitive framework, with due regard to legislative and regulatory provisions applying to concentration, collusion, combines, restraints of trade, price fixing, etc.

The advertising profession, while emphasizing the essentiality of the persuasive character of advertising, appears to be recognizing a trend in consumer demand for increasing the informative content of advertising messages. To quote a former President of the American Association of Advertising Agencies, Inc.: "It is probable that advertising will become increasingly informative, because that's what consumers want, and that's what turns out to be most effective with them."[6] (See also Chapter 7.)

The views then differ as to whether a distinction between the "informative" and "persuasive" content of advertising is meaningful and practical. Professor Johnson suggests that "only a

---

4 *The Canadian Quandary, op. cit.,* p. 280.
5 *Advertising, A New Approach,* by Walter Taplin, Little, Brown and Company, Boston, 1963, p. 77.
6 "The Peculiar Responsibility of the Consumer", Address by John Crichton, at Adcraft Club of Detroit, October 2, 1964, p. 8.

relatively small part of advertising can be classed as primarily 'persuasive' rather than primarily 'informative' ".[7]

Since it cannot be denied that advertising by businessmen aims at consumer acceptance of their products—though the persuasive character of the advertising message may be subtle and not immediately apparent—the burden of proof of the practicability and usefulness of the concept for policy formulation rests with the proponents of the distinction between the "informative" and "persuasive" contents of advertising.

Purpose of Advertising

The purpose of advertising, from the point of view of business, is to enable the consumer to decide whether he wishes to purchase a particular commodity and, if possible, to persuade him to buy the commodity offered for sale by the advertiser. Thus advertising is an essential part of the selling efforts of business.

Having said that advertising is an aid to, and in fact a part of selling, it should not be identified with other types of sales efforts such as promotion through free samples, trading stamps, consumer contests, etc.

Advertising uses certain mass media and is thus one of the most economic means of reaching a large number of consumers in a highly industrialized society. The most successful type of advertising is the kind that tells its story effectively to the consumer and enables him to make up his mind. Businessmen have learned that if an advertising message becomes too overwhelming in its efforts to persuade, it may be rejected by the consumer as being in bad taste or irrational and thus defeat its purpose.

Promotional efforts, other than advertising, of the type that have found increasing consumer acceptance in recent years, appeal to the "play" instinct of the general public, and this covers a variety of situations—the feeling "of getting something for nothing" through trading stamps, the winning of a "prize in a

---

7 *The Canadian Quandary, op. cit.,* p. 282.

contest", etc. Such promotional campaigns are the result, so it is claimed, of excessive competition—an effort to take the business away from a competitor at whatever the cost and by whatever means. The public apparently is condoning such practices, for if it did not, businessmen would soon abandon such practices as uneconomic and as a waste of money.

As one executive of a chain-store explained: "We have trading-stamps because the housewife wants them." Or as a witness representing a drug company before the Royal Commission on Health Services testified: "Promotional costs of drugs are high, but without them we would not sell our drugs. If our competitors would cut down promotional costs, we would do the same."

Advertising replaced to a large extent an earlier type of selling effort—personal selling—for the simple reason that it was more economic and became gradually more effective with the development of mass communication media, particularly television.

In Chapter 4, evidence is presented, showing that the rate of growth in advertising expenditures has slowed down significantly in the last five years, expanding at a slower rate than Gross National Product, personal disposable income and consumer expenditures. Since the value of goods and services sold to consumers has increased more rapidly than advertising expenditures, the question arises whether in prosperous periods a relatively lesser amount of selling effort is required, or whether a shift may be underway in the manner of selling.

While there is no quantitative evidence available to measure the growing importance of the "gimmick" type of sales promotion, the fact that it has spread so widely and continues to enjoy consumer acceptance is suggestive of the possibility that such a shift in the techniques of selling is in fact taking place. This is another area that could usefully be subjected to further enquiry and measurement.

For, while advertising carries a large informative content and thus helps consumers in making a choice on the basis of criteria he may value, such as quality, service and price, the same cannot be claimed to be the case for the "gimmick" type of promotion. For this type of selling, it is claimed, appeals to the baser instincts of humanity, and whether this represents a socially useful function, is a question for the moralists to decide.

As to the future direction which promotional activities may take, Professor Taplin suggests that they may represent a transitional phase from heavy advertising to reliance on greater price competition. He describes these promotional techniques as "neither pure advertising nor pure price competition". He considers them as a separate form comprising a "particularly unstable third category". He concludes: "They (promotional devices) amount to price competition in disguise, or indicators of a phase of transition away from advertising and toward price competition—a movement . . . which certainly indicates a shift of emphasis."[8]

To come back to the point that advertising assists businessmen in their selling efforts. This is only part of the purpose of advertising. It also assists the consumer by providing him with an opportunity to choose between alternatives—a service which he is willing to pay for in a wealthy society like Canada's.

Professor Johnson explains the relationship between wealth and consumer choice in these terms:

> Wealth, or high income, is synonymous with having a wide range of choice; choice involves the necessity of decision; and decision requires information and advice about the alternatives available, for time is short and the alternatives are many. Wealth also implies that basic needs are satisfied, so that money can be afforded to pay for information, to gratify psychologically and sociologically oriented wants as well as physiological wants, and to experiment with different objects of expenditure. Rising wealth implies a steady widening of the available range of choice, and the necessity of decisions about how the increasing

---

8 *Advertising, A New Approach, op. cit.*, pp. 122 and 123.

capacity for choice is to be utilized again involving a need for information and advice about alternatives.

The average consumer, however, confronted with the need for a multiplicity of decisions each of which is typically of relatively small importance to him, has neither the capacity nor the patience to assemble for himself the information and advice he requires, or to assimilate it if he could assemble it. Nor have consumers—at least until recently—generally found it attractive or feasible to band together to assemble the relevant information. . . . Instead, the task of providing information and advice has been assumed by the sellers of goods and services, as part of their self-interested efforts to sell their wares. Unlike consumers, producers and distributors have the financial resources and the commercial incentive to assemble and disseminate information about what they have to sell, recouping the cost from the prices they receive from their goods. From the standpoint of the individual consumer the system has the advantage of pooling the cost of information and yet enabling him to avoid paying for information and advice he does not want. Its disadvantages are that in some circumstances the charge for information may be excessive and inescapable, and that the advice may be bad advice.[9]

Thus, advertising—and the reference here is to advertising addressed to the consumer only—serves two purposes: (1) it meets the need of businessmen in selling their product or service in the most economic manner at their disposal; and (2) it assists the consumer to make as rational a choice as is possible in purchasing a product or a service on the basis of information available to him, without paying for this service until he buys the good or service, since the advertising costs are incorporated in the final sales price.

So far, the reference has been to advertising in highly industrialized and developed countries. But advertising has also a significant role to play in societies less well off than those of North America and Western Europe. For in these countries, advertising can help people to envision the benefits that may accrue to them from acquiring increasing skills and additional

---

9 *The Canadian Quandary, op. cit.,* pp. 270 and 271.

education, and the use of such human improvements for productive ends. The economist speaks of the "demonstration effect", that is the creation of incentives through demonstrating what other people and nations have been able to achieve through scientific advances and efficient use of available resources, of which human beings are the most important ones.

Advertising through the effective use of mass communication media can make a major contribution to assist emerging nations in speeding up their economic development and enlighten people on the necessity of their wholehearted support for the cause of social progress. Here is a new role for advertising that has hardly been grasped.

Effect of Advertising

Advertising achieves economic meaning or economic effect in two ways.

One is the direct employment that is created in the advertising industry resulting from the spending made by advertisers. The advertising industry provides a service and employs people working in advertising agencies, in communication media and a host of ancillary occupations. That number of people in relation to Canada's total labour force is quite small, involving a fraction of one per cent (see Chapter 14).

The other, and far more important, effect of advertising is the contribution it makes to assist Canadian businessmen to sell the sum total of goods and services they produce. In its broadest aggregate, this sum total is represented by the Gross National Product, which for 1966 was estimated at about $57½ billion.

Use of advertising by business may contribute to an increase in the sales of goods and services, both in total for the firm and for particular items. The producers and distributors of such goods and services, in turn, provide employment and income to those engaged in creating them. Thus the making of advertising expenditures contributes to Gross National Product the sum total of all goods and services in a country in a given period of time, both directly through the incomes earned by those engaged in providing the services, and indirectly by facilitating sales of output produced, which in turn entails increases in earnings to factors of production involved.

To add to this summary, using one of Professor Johnson's facetious remarks that has a substantive bearing on the subject:

> There is no more sickening demonstration of the capacity of advertising men to fall victim to their own techniques of obfuscation than the spectacle of an advertising man standing up before an audience of housewives, placing his hand on what in a normal human being would pass for a heart, and solemnly assuring his audience that if it were not for advertising all their husbands would be on relief. The fact that in Canada and the United States in recent years an unusually high proportion of the husbands has been on relief anyway, in spite of mounting advertising expenditures, is never mentioned.[10]

Professor Johnson concludes that the argument that advertising creates a market providing "employment for workers who would otherwise be unemployed" is untenable.[11] In other words, advertising does not add to increasing aggregate demand for goods and services. For if it did, it would contribute to increasing production—allowing for changes in inventories—and this in turn would lead to increasing levels in employment and income. It is not that Professor Johnson's views on this point are accepted by all economists, but they are accepted by many.

Forms of Advertising

Advertising involves the purchase of space in printed media or time on broadcast media. In this manner, advertisers address their advertising messages to audiences which are circumscribed by the coverage area of the communication media. The latter may include the readers of newspapers, the listeners of radio and the viewers of television. The advertiser has no say in the

---

10 *Ibid.*, p. 292.
11 *Ibid.*

editorial content of a newspaper,[12] and little influence on broadcast media programming. Rather, the advertiser chooses the media and the type of advertising that will obtain for him the maximum exposure of potential customers to his sales efforts. Advertising takes three forms:

1. The visual presentation, mainly the printed word or picture. This covers advertising in newspapers, periodicals, other printed media including catalogues, direct mail, etc., and outdoor advertising including billboards, car cards, etc. Advertising in printed media is the oldest form of advertising since the arrival of the mass media, and particularly so in Canada since the beginning of the twentieth century.

2. The oral presentation, and this covers mainly radio advertising. This form of presenting commercial messages became popular in the 1920's, suffered like other forms of advertising during the 1930's and World War II, and expanded rapidly in the immediate post-World War II years, with the rate of growth slowing down after 1952 when television was introduced in Canada.

3. The combination of visual and oral presentation, with television advertising the newest and so far the most rapidly growing means of communicating commercial messages to the consuming public.

It was the growth of mass media that made advertising so effective, in part because it offered a more economic means in reaching the public and in part because it was able to reach the widest possible audiences, a point developed further as the study

---

12 "The surest way to lose the interest of that audience, and thus undermine the value of the advertiser's investment, would be for the advertisers or the advertising agencies to try to influence the nature of contents, directly or indirectly. The dividing line between editorial authority and integrity and paid advertising content is very clearly defined, and fiercely guarded by the editorial staff"; and the advertising profession respects "that distinction, as a matter of principle and as a matter of good business." (See *Proceedings* of the Special Joint Committee of the Senate and House of Commons on Consumer Credit (Prices), December 13, 1966, p. 1999.)

proceeds. At the same time, advertising contributed significantly to the growth of media through an ever-increasing utilization of the communication services the media have to offer.

Coverage of Advertising

There are in the main three types of advertising coverage:

1. National coverage. This coverage is designed to reach the general public across the nation or an entire industry, trade or profession. Such advertising is usually placed in publications with nationwide appeal and readership, and on radio and television networks.

2. Local coverage. Such coverage is designed to reach people in a particular community. This type of advertising may be originating either locally (for example, by a local business firm trying to attract local consumers), or it may be a supplement to national advertising aimed at creating buying impulses for products and services advertised nationally. Local advertising is placed in local newspapers, local radio and television stations, outdoor advertising, localized direct mail, etc.

3. "Selective" coverage. This coverage relates to local purchases of time or space designed to reach a larger audience across the country in particular markets. For example, an advertiser might buy a program of some public appeal which he will then endeavour to place with a number of individual stations to build up a desired audience.

Having explained in this chapter what advertising is, the next question is: Does advertising provide a useful service to the consumer, to business and to society as a whole? What are its advantages and disadvantages? These questions are dealt with in general terms in Chapters 2 and 3, with some specific aspects covered in subsequent chapters.

2

Advantages

Balancing Advantages Against Disadvantages

There is a growing body of literature on the merits and demerits of advertising, and more recently comments by the economic profession on the need to balance the beneficial results of advertising against its adverse consequences, thus assessing the *net* effects of advertising on economic progress and optimum allocation of resources.

Little purpose would be served by reviewing the main literature on the subject, particularly since a good part of it is repetitive, except insofar as it bears on the specific points selected for examination in this study. It may, however, assist the reader to have at his disposal a listing of some of the benefits that may accrue to society as a result of advertising, as claimed by its defenders and in part admitted by some of its critics.

Such a list is presented below, with footnote references to the sources of the claims made, so that the reader can refer to the original material if he so wishes.

List of Advantages

Advertising may

1. decrease the cost of selling
2. lower the cost of production
3. lower prices to the consumer
4. aid in the education of the general public
5. aid in stabilizing production
6. aid in standardizing production
7. aid in improving quality
8. aid in simplifying products
9. help in preventing fluctuations in prices[1]
10. increase investment
11. advance technology
12. raise real national income
13. reduce risks in new ventures
14. pave the way for the product imitator and his lower priced private-brand products[2]
15. increase scale of operations
16. widen consumer choice
17. increase variety of goods marketed
18. encourage innovations
19. speed up returns on investment to business
20. stimulate product and industrial diversification
21. reduce amount of retail sales effort required per unit of retail sales
22. replace a more economic for a less economic selling technique
23. subsidize mass communication media providing essential services to consumers[3]

---

[1] Items 1-9 are included in *Market Analysis—Advertising and Advertising Mediums*, Publication by the U.S. Chamber of Commerce, Washington, D.C., 1925.

[2] Items 10-14 are from "The Economic Effects of Advertising", by Neil H. Borden, in *Mass Communications*, edited by Wilbur Schramm, University of Illinois Press, Urbana, 1960, pp. 251 ff.

[3] Items 15-23 are based in part on Prof. Borden's work, referred to above, and in part on elaboration by David M. Blank, in "Some Comments on the Role of Advertising in the American Economy—

(Footnote continued on next page)

24. provide information to consumers
25. bring buyers and sellers together
26. increase competition[4]
27. add to the consumer's stock of knowledge
28. provide the consumer with a service by saving him time and trouble in finding out for himself
29. give consumer confidence in brand-name products[5]
30. increase the capacity of choice of the consumer
31. assist in a "pooling" of costs to consumers
32. contribute to improvement in the standard of living
33. contribute to the sharing of opulence among the masses[6]
34. contribute to mass production
35. contribute to mass consumption
36. encourage research and development
37. facilitate the exercise of free choice and free will
38. represent an essential factor in the new economics of abundance[7]
39. advance the frontiers of demand
40. add new and interesting experiences to life
41. reduce the trial and error approach on the part of the consumer
42. develop new buying habits[8]
43. not produce a "link" between advertising intensity and price increases[9]

A Plea for Revaluation", Paper at Meetings of the American Marketing Association, Chicago, December 28, 1964, Reprint, pp. 7-11.

[4] Items 24-26 are from "Advertising and Competition", by Donald F. Turner, Paper at the Briefing Conference on Federal Controls of Advertising and Promotion, sponsored by the Federal Bar Association, etc., Washington, D.C., June 2, 1966, p. 1.

[5] Items 27-29 are from "Supply and Demand for Advertising Messages", op. cit., pp. 462-464.

[6] Items 30-33 are from The Canadian Quandary, op. cit., pp. 270, 271, 280 and 293.

[7] Items 34-38 are from "The Social and Economic Context of Advertising", op. cit., pp. 3, 5 and 6.

[8] Items 39-42 are from Advertising, A New Approach, op. cit., pp. 117 and 127.

[9] Item 43 is from "Advertising and Competition", Preliminary Report, by Dr. Jules Backman, 57th A.N.A. Annual Meeting, Colorado Springs, October 23-26, 1966, p. 10.

Further Enquiry Needed

This listing involves overlapping in many respects; furthermore, it is not complete. What this listing of claims of the benefits of advertising suggests, however, is that there is no lack of enthusiasm or restraint on the part of some exponents in overstating the "good" or "constructive" contribution of advertising to the modern way of life.

Except for a few professional writers, most of the other claims put forward are based on conjecture and inherent belief that, if anything helps the competitive system as it now operates in North America, it must be "good". The fact that there is a growing body of opinion which holds that "excessive" advertising and monopolistic and oligopolistic practices supported by large volume advertising may contribute to interference with the principle of the "best" obtainable resource allocation,[10] as well as with the working of the competitive system in a free enterprise society, is frequently overlooked. Nor is there much effort devoted to finding out what the facts are. There is hardly any vital field of economic endeavour that has been so grossly neglected in Canada, as in some other countries, as research concerning the role and impact of advertising.

What goes under the name "research" are market surveys, consumer attitude surveys, newspaper readers, radio listeners and television viewers measurement surveys—all tools necessary for the day-to-day operations and in the planning of advertising campaigns of large business corporations and their advisers, the advertising agencies. But when it comes to measuring and assessing the effects of advertising on the economy in all its ramifications, very little is done in Canada, a point developed further in Chapter 18 and in the Appendix.

---

[10] The concept of "best" obtainable resource allocation is used here as a practical alternative to a theoretical "optimum" allocation of resources.

3

Disadvantages

Criticism of Advertising

Although the critics of advertising have been increasing in numbers in recent years, the number of arguments they have been advancing are not as numerous as those advanced by proponents of advertising, though at times they are better documented.

But the evidence so far presented by both the defenders and the critics of advertising is inconclusive. Some of it is controversial and subject to different interpretations. Much more examination and marshalling of evidence is needed before adequate judgment can be formulated about the merits and demerits of advertising, and the net effect on social welfare and economic progress. It is not enough to say that advertising, on balance, serves a constructive purpose and is overwhelmingly endorsed by society. There is also need to recite chapter and verse to disprove the claims of the doubters.

The critics of advertising list these disadvantages:

List of Disadvantages

Advertising may
1. misinform the consumer
2. change the pattern of preferences of the consumer
3. contain deceptive messages
4. concentrate on persuasion rather than on information
5. involve a waste of resources[1]
6. contribute to "more concentrated market structures"
7. impose "unacceptable restraints on competition"
8. lead to "the establishment of high monopolistic prices"
9. reduce entry opportunities of new firms
10. lead to particularly high monopolistic profits[2]
11. protect "producers' market shares"
12. contribute to wasteful product differentiation of a minute kind
13. contribute to cost increases[3]
14. involve "more advertising foisted off on them (consumers)" than necessary or desirable
15. antagonize consumers[4]
16. encourage the "wrong" type of consumption
17. affect adversely the cost of living
18. create conflicts between the interests of the advertising originators and the advertising media
19. create "sensational" journalism
20. create "sensational" television
21. contribute to increasing "private consumption" at the expense of "public provision of collective goods and services"

---

[1] Items 1-5 are from *American Industry: Structure, Conduct, Performance*, by Richard Caves, Prentice-Hall Inc., Englewood Cliffs, N.J., 1964, p. 102.

[2] Items 6-10 are from "Advertising and Competition", *op. cit.*, pp. 2 and 3.

[3] Items 11-13 are from "Some Comments on the Role of Advertising in the American Economy—A Plea for Revaluation", *op. cit.*, pp. 3-5.

[4] Item 14 is from "Supply and Demand for Advertising Messages", *op. cit.*, p. 457.

Item 15 is from *Dynamic Marketing Behaviour*, by Wroe Alderson, R. D. Irwin Inc., Homewood, Illinois, 1965, p. 129.

22. offend the esthetic and moral standards
23. contribute to cyclical variations
24. emphasize "the gross material pleasures of life"
25. use "propaganda" means to persuade consumers[5]
26. raise distribution costs
27. reduce consumer choice in product fields in which brand preferences have been established
28. encourage "competition in advertising and other non-price forms" at the expense of product quality and price competition
29. affect adversely consumer valuations
30. contribute to price rigidity[6]
31. encourage the purchase of useless trappings, e.g. unnecessary packaging
32. contribute to "excessive" competition
33. bring about a misallocation of a nation's limited resources[7]

Is Advertising Necessary?

As in the case of listing the advantages of advertising, the above enumeration involves overlapping critical comments without covering the subject fully. But perhaps one useful conclusion can be drawn from comparing an enumeration of the advantages with an enumeration of the disadvantages of advertising: this is that there is hardly any other area of economic activity where the gulf between speaking well and speaking ill of an industry is as wide as in the case of advertising.

Looking at the literature over the last several years, the voices of the professional critics are becoming stronger. And

---

5 Items 16-25 are from *The Canadian Quandary, op. cit.,* pp. 273-275 and 282. The reference to the contribution to advertising as a disturbing factor in achieving a social balance between private and public goods goes back to the writing of J. K. Galbraith in *The Affluent Society.*
6 Items 26-30 are from "The Economic Effects of Advertising", *op. cit.,* pp. 260, 280, 283 and 288.
7 Items 31-33 are from *Broadcast Advertising in Canada, Past and Future Growth,* by O. J. Firestone, University of Ottawa Press, Ottawa, 1966, p. 24.

looking at newspaper reports, the voices of the public are being heard more frequently and louder, and this in turn has aroused the legislature and Government to look further into the question whether the kind of advertising practices currently in vogue serve the consumer well or whether there are areas where the public interest may be adversely affected.

Increasingly, the question is being asked: Is advertising necessary? Does it perform a socially useful and essential function?

Even the critics of advertising admit that some advertising is necessary in a market-oriented type of economy. Some suggest that "informative" advertising is socially desirable (see Chapter 1), while others say that certain quantities and certain types of advertising involve a productive use of resources. But, when advertising expenditures are very large, to the extent that it has become customary in North America, with the bulk of all advertising undertaken by a small group of major corporations, and with the prospects of further substantial increases in such spending over the next decade, then critics say that there is a point where advertising becomes excessive and wasteful, and hence socially undesirable.

In this context, the question as to whether advertising is a necessary and desirable use of scarce resources, revolves around four points:

(a) the amount of advertising
(b) the type of advertising
(c) the objective of advertising
(d) the effect of advertising.

To deal with the first point, the question is: When do advertising expenditures become "too large"? Should the advertising budget be related to the size of a corporation? Should it be related to the types of commodities advertised? Should it be related to the number of new products to be promoted? Should it be related to the changing competitive position of a firm? Should Government set a limit to the amount of advertising a firm could spend through direct control and regulation? Or should Government keep advertising within given limits through fiscal devices such as a tax disincentive for advertising expenditures made above a set proportion of sales? Or should market forces be allowed to determine the extent and the economics of promotional efforts pursued by business?

The difficulty arises because all advertising expenditures, both small and large, serve an economic purpose. For, if they did not, efficient management—always looking for economies— would not authorize such expenditures. As Richard B. Tennant observes:

> Even large advertising expenditures may perform an essential function in bringing goods to market with a smaller total resource commitment than if other distributive devices were employed.

> This conclusion is obscured not only by the preconceptions and mental sets of many lawyers and economists, but also by some analytical devices in economics that sometimes delude economists themselves and that appear to have been responsible for a good bit of the unsupportable folklore about advertising among lawyers.[8]

On the second point, misleading or offensive advertising is objectionable. Little advertising appears to fall into this category in Canada, with the bulk of advertising being formulated of a generally acceptable quality. This state of affairs has been brought about in part as a result of public regulations, and to an even greater extent as a result of industrial and professional observance of standards of behaviour. To quote the Institute of Canadian Advertising:

---

8 "Advertising, Competition and the Antitrust Laws, An Economist's View", by Richard B. Tennant, Paper given at Symposium sponsored by the Subcommittee on Regulations Affecting Advertising of the Committee on the Federal Trade Commission Act, Annual Meeting of the Section of Antitrust Law, American Bar Association, New York, August 10, 1964, p. 171.

Advertising agencies, advertisers and all major media also subscribe to the Canadian Code of Advertising Standards, designed to insure that advertising is prepared in such a way as to respect the tastes and interests of the public at large.[9]

On the third point, the objective of advertising may be informative or persuasive or both. A major portion of advertising falls into the latter category. For example, a recent survey of advertising in two daily newspapers showed that 2,091 out of 4,157 classified advertisements included "selling" phrases.[10] In other words, just about one half of the advertisements combined "informative" and "persuasive" content. In the case of broadcast and magazine advertising, the proportion of advertisements with persuasive content would be considerably greater.

This point was elaborated earlier in Chapter 1, with the presentation of different views held by some economists about the social undesirability of the "persuasive" type of advertising, and the strong view held by the advertising profession about the essential character of such advertising to further economic growth and general welfare in Canada.

On the fourth point, a great deal of criticism about advertising expenditures made in Canada being "too large" centre around the effect that such "excessive" spending may have under certain circumstances and in certain combinations on limiting competition through encouraging industrial concentration and restraint of trade.

Problems of Concentration

This leads to the question of concentration of industry and the use of large-scale advertising as a means of reducing competition and supporting price maintenance. While enquiries in this

---

[9] *Proceedings* of the Special Joint Committee of the Senate and House of Commons on Consumer Credit (Prices), December 13, 1966, p. 2005.
[10] *Ibid.*, p. 2009.

area have been limited in Canada[11], a considerable amount of literature has been built up in the United States. Without in any way attempting to summarize the arguments or the material available, the inconclusiveness of the evidence presented in the United States may be noted.

The argument revolves mainly around the question whether advertising hinders competition or not, particularly large-scale advertising undertaken by the giant corporations in the United States. The anti-competitive effects that have been advanced have been summarized by Professor Jules Backman as follows:

1. The large company has the power of the large purse which enables it to spend substantial sums on advertising, particularly to implement product differentiation.
2. Advertising thus creates a barrier to new firms entering industry.
3. The result is greater economic concentration.
4. Because of their protected position, these firms charge monopolistic prices.
5. High monopolistic prices in turn result in excessively larger profits.[12]

Willard Mueller, the Chief Economist for the U.S. Federal Trade Commission observed: "It seems probable that advertising-created and maintained product differentiation constitutes the chief barrier confronting prospective entrants in many grocery product industries."[13]

---

11 One example of a study that bears in part on the subject is *Discriminatory Pricing Practices in the Grocery Trade,* Material collected under Section 42 of the Combines Investigation Act, Department of Justice, Queen's Printer, Ottawa, 1958, pp. 181 and 194 ff. See also evidence on "Statutory Provisions with Respect to Promotional Activities", given by Mr. J. A. Scollin of the Criminal Law Section, Department of Justice, *Proceedings* of the Special Joint Committee of the Senate and House of Commons on Consumer Credit (Prices), February 9, 1967.

12 "Advertising and Competition", *op. cit.,* p. 1.

13 "Processor vs. Distributor Brands in Food Distribution", Address by Willard Mueller, the National Council of Farm Cooperatives, Houston, Texas, January 13, 1964, p. 5e.

Donald F. Turner, the Assistant Attorney General in Charge of the Antitrust Division of the U.S. Department of Justice, noted in a recent speech that one factor contributing to industrial concentration and reduction in competition was the difficulty of entry of new firms created "as a result of the barriers created through extensive advertising".[14]

The defenders of advertising make three points:

1. The claim that advertising is a significant factor in industrial concentration has not been proven. To illustrate: Professor Telser of the University of Chicago, who has conducted a comprehensive statistical analysis of the relationship between the intensity of advertising and economic concentration, concluded: "The correlation between concentration and advertising is unimpressive."[15]

2. The suggestion that advertising contributes to raising prices and thus to inflation is not supported in overall terms by the postwar experience in the United States. Professor Jules Backman of New York University has undertaken a number of studies examining the advertising-sales ratios for 1962 and price changes between 1947 and 1965, covering both wholesale and retail prices. Professor Backman recently gave a progress report based on the studies in which he and his associates are engaged. He observed:

> There is no support for the assumption that the industries with intensive advertising had such a degree of market power that they increased prices substantially during the postwar price inflation. On the contrary, there was a tendency for the least intensive advertisers to have the larger increases in prices.[16]

3. The claim that industries with high advertising expenditures tend to earn considerably higher profit rates than industries making smaller advertising efforts appears to be not

---

[14] "Advertising and Competition", *op. cit.*, p. 3.
[15] "Advertising and Competition", by Lester G. Telser, *The Journal of Political Economy*, December 1964, pp. 542-544.
[16] "Advertising and Competition", *op. cit.*, p. 9.

in accordance with the results obtained from some research studies.

Professor Backman, in another examination of the experiences of 125 corporations representing the largest advertisers in the United States found "that less than one-tenth of the differences in rates of return is explained by the differences in the advertising-sales ratio." Professor Backman further reported:

> The average return on invested capital for 105 manufacturing companies with the largest dollar expenditures for advertising was 13.6% in 1964. This compares with 12.6% for 2,298 leading manufacturing companies reported by the First National City Bank of New York. These modest differences in profit returns are not necessarily all attributable to the effects of advertising. At the most it can be said that companies with the *largest dollar expenditures* for advertising reported profits that were 1.0 percentage point higher than the average for leading manufacturing companies.[17]

Professor Backman concluded:

> The barrier to entry created by large financial requirements is weak. The relationship between advertising intensity and high economic concentration is non-existent. There appears to be no link between advertising intensity and price increases. Intensive advertisers appear to have only moderately higher profit rates than other companies. The record shows clearly that advertising is highly competitive, not anti-competitive.[18]

But the case does not rest here. The studies undertaken by Professor Backman and his associates have to be completed. The proponents of the claim that large-scale advertising may affect adversely competitive conditions in the United States are insisting on further enquiries and studies being undertaken, including proceedings under the U.S. Anti-Trust Provisions.

It will take time and patient study to come up with some acceptable answers to these puzzling questions raised by the

---

[17] *Ibid.*, p. 10.
[18] *Ibid.*

controversy about the economic effects of advertising, particularly its effects on competition, costs and prices. Such studies are underway in the United States. The question arises: is there need for similar studies to be undertaken in Canada? If so, what form should such studies take and what agencies of business and government might be most appropriately concerned with them? These questions are dealt with in part in the remainder of this chapter and in part in Chapter 18, where an outline for a Canadian research program in the field of the economic effects of advertising is presented.

Canadian Enquiry

On March 22, 1965, the Canadian Government asked the Economic Council of Canada to launch a broad examination into prices, costs, incomes, and productivity, and their relationship to sustain economic growth. The terms of reference of the enquiry were as follows:

> 1. To study factors affecting price determination and the interrelation between movements in prices and costs and levels of productivity and incomes.
> 2. To report on their relationship to sustained economic growth and to the achievement of high levels of employment and trade and rising standards of living.
> 3. To review the policies and experiences of other countries in this field and their relevance for Canada.[19]

In November 1966, the Economic Council of Canada submitted its Third Review. It devoted three chapters to the problems of inflation. In compliance with the terms of reference, mentioned above, the Council dealt in its report with the process of what it called "partial inflation", price goals and productivity problems, the sensitivity of the Canadian economy to developments abroad, the general features of price and cost experiences in Canada since 1949 including cyclical behaviour of prices, effects of exchange rate adjustments and of indirect

---

[19] *House of Commons Debates*, Queen's Printer, Ottawa, March 22, 1965, p. 12621.

taxes, and a comparison with price trends in the United States. Other factors affecting price changes included collective bargaining and business pricing.

In discussing price setting by large business corporations in Canada, the Council made no reference to the effect of advertising and its role as a cost factor in price determination. The Council concluded this particular assessment by saying that, generally, "it is difficult to distinguish clearly the influence of discretionary price-making by large firms from the rest of the complex forces which play on prices and costs, especially in an open economy such as Canada's."[20] This conclusion is in line with the results obtained from a number of American studies which emphasize the difficulties of separating one or the other factor for such a complex mechanism as price setting in a competitive society.

The Economic Council of Canada further dealt with "trade offs" between rates of price changes and rates of unemployment, and with the policy implications inherent in an economic situation marked by "partial inflation", taking into account incomes policies and other measures adopted in other countries facing similar problems to those experienced in Canada.

As mentioned earlier, the Council made no reference to advertising as a contributing factor to price rises. Nor did it put forward the suggestion that excessive advertising could be a factor and that this would be a matter that deserved further examination.

It is quite possible that the lack of evidence linking increases in advertising expenditures to increases in prices during a period of cyclical expansion may explain the absence of a reference in the discussion of factors contributing to inflationary pressures in Canada in recent years. If this is part of the explanation, the Council may view changes of advertising expenditures and

---

20 *Prices, Productivity and Employment*, Economic Council of Canada, Third Annual Review, Queen's Printer, Ottawa, November 1966, p. 136.

the use of advertising as a means to increase market power, less as a cyclical factor and more as a factor affecting economic growth over the longer term.

The Economic Council of Canada did in fact make reference to the problems of market power and the need for consumer protection and it emphasized the desirability of continuing study of this subject. To quote:

> While it (market power) appears to have been a factor of some importance in Canada, it cannot readily be assigned sole or principal responsibility for the kind of rising price phenomena which the economy typically experiences as it moves through a business-cycle expansion. There is too much evidence of the influence on prices of other important forces such as increases in aggregate demand and foreign price changes. The climate of expectations is also of great significance. A major analytical difficulty, which has not yet been surmounted, is that of disentangling the *independent* influence of market power from these other forces.[21]

The undertaking of a study in this field has now been authorized by the Canadian Government. Terms of reference of the enquiry were announced on July 22, 1966, as follows:

> In the light of the Government's long-term economic objectives, to study and advise regarding:
>
> (a) the interests of the consumer particularly as they relate to the functions of the Department of the Registrar General;
> (b) combines, mergers, monopolies and restraint of trade;
> (c) patents, trade-marks, copyrights and registered industrial designs.[22]

It would appear quite appropriate that the Economic Council of Canada, as part of the scope of the new enquiry, consider the economic implications of advertising, with particular reference to the claims that are being made—so far largely unsubstantiated in Canada—that substantial increases in advertising

---

21 *Ibid.*, p. 180.
22 *Press Release*, the President of the Privy Council, The Honourable Guy Favreau, Q.C., Ottawa, July 22, 1966.

expenditures have been a significant factor in the creation of market power and in industrial concentration, with corresponding ill-effects on consumer choices and consumer prices.

Out of the deliberations and studies conducted by the Economic Council of Canada may evolve recommendations to the Government which could lead to a broader, more economic and less legalistic approach being made in Canada in the use of the provisions of the Combines Investigation Act.

4

Expenditures

Coverage of Advertising Expenditures

Advertisers place commercial messages with communication media. They pay for the services of the media by making advertising expenditures.

When advertisers spend money on advertising, some of it may go directly to communication media. Some of it will go to advertising agencies which perform in the main advisory, planning and research functions for their clients.[1]

---

[1] The main services to business performed by advertising agencies have been summarized in these terms:
  (a) Assistance in formulating and executing advertising campaigns and testing their effectiveness.
  (b) Assistance in marketing the products of their clients including studies of the products involved, their sales appeal, their marketability, their competitiveness, etc.
  (c) Assistance in developing a favourable corporate or industrial image in relation to:
      (i) the consuming public,
      (ii) employees of the company,
      (iii) distributing organizations (e.g. dealerships), and
      (iv) governments.
  (d) Assistance in advertising market and product research.
  (See *Broadcast Advertising in Canada, Past and Future Growth, op. cit.*, p. 13.)

Advertising agencies are currently looking after about one-half of the total advertising placed by industry and governments, with the rest of the business placed directly by advertisers. The trend is for more of the business to be placed through advertising agencies.

Advertising agencies are paid a commission for their service —usually 15 per cent of gross billings. Since about one-half of total advertising goes through the hands of advertising agencies, between 7 and 7½ per cent of total advertising expenditures made in Canada are represented by the revenues of advertising agencies. With total advertising expenditures involving $821 million in 1966, net advertising expenditures (that is, after deducting advertising agency commissions) are placed at $766 million (preliminary estimate).

The latter, while representing a net figure from the advertisers' point of view, represents a gross figure to the communication media, for these media, in turn, incur selling expenses. They employ staff to do the selling for them or they engage sales agencies to do the selling. In the broadcasting field, these sales agencies are called "rep" houses. These are "firms specializing in the sale of broadcast advertising on radio and television stations. Thus they are sales agents acting on behalf of broadcasting stations with most of their sales involving national advertising. 'Rep' houses also do some local selling for some stations but the majority of stations handle such sales with their own sales staff."[2]

Advertising Expenditures and Revenues of Communication Media

Revenues from advertising represent the bulk of income received by privately owned communication media. The proportion will vary depending on the type of media. In the case of broadcasting, the proportion is higher than in print media.

---

2 *Ibid.*, p. 104.

This can be illustrated by data available for 1963. In that year advertising revenues of newspapers and periodicals amounted to $309 million and sales of newspapers and periodicals to $103 million. Thus the latter comprised about 25 per cent of the total.[3] In the same year, the ratio of revenues of broadcasting media from the sale of other than broadcasting time, that is for advertising purposes, to total revenues varied between 5 and 14 per cent, depending on the definition of production income.[4]

Trends in Gross Advertising Expenditures

Over the last twenty years, advertising expenditures (gross) have been rising continuously, as the Canadian economy expanded. This expansion continued also through the several recessionary periods which Canada has experienced since the end of World War II (see Chapter 6).

Advertising expenditures rose more rapidly than general economic activity, as measured by Gross National Product, a subject discussed further on. But the rate of growth has varied.

In the first five years after the end of World War II, 1946-1951, advertising expenditures about doubled as business, institutions and governments made increasing use of advertising from the reduced level of advertising activity that had become a necessity as a result of the exigencies of World War II and the immediate postwar period (see Table 1).

In the next five year period, 1951-1956, advertising expenditures rose by 77 per cent, still at a substantial rate. One of the reasons was the rapid expansion of the Canadian economy, spurred on by the heavy demand for goods and services as a result of the Korean War. Other reasons included a multitude of new consumer goods coming on the market, including such

---

[3] *Printing, Publishing and Allied Industries, 1963,* Dominion Bureau of Statistics, Ottawa, May 1966, p. 56.
[4] *Broadcast Advertising in Canada, Past and Future Growth, op. cit.,* p. 287.

TABLE 1

GROSS NATIONAL PRODUCT AND ADVERTISING EXPENDITURES,
TOTAL AND PER CAPITA, CANADA AND THE UNITED STATES,
1946-1966

Year	CANADA				UNITED STATES			
	GROSS NATIONAL PRODUCT ($ millions)	ADVERTISING EXPENDITURES*			GROSS NATIONAL PRODUCT ($ millions)	ADVERTISING EXPENDITURES		
		Total ($ millions)	Per Capita (dollars)	Total as Percentage of G.N.P.		Total ($ millions)	Per Capita (dollars)	Total as Percentage of G.N.P.
1946	11,850	130.9	10.65	1.1	208.5	3,364	23.70	1.6
1947	13,165	158.4	12.62	1.2	231.3	4,260	29.44	1.8
1948	15,120	183.1	14.28	1.2	257.6	4,864	33.04	1.9
1949	16,343	211.1	15.70	1.3	256.5	5,202	34.73	2.0
1950	18,006	234.0	17.07	1.3	284.8	5,710	37.50	2.0
1951	21,170	262.3	18.72	1.2	328.4	6,426	41.49	2.0
1952	23,995	292.3	20.22	1.2	345.5	7,156	45.42	2.1
1953	25,020	331.4	22.32	1.3	364.6	7,809	48.75	2.1
1954	24,871	363.4	23.77	1.5	364.8	8,164	50.08	2.2
1955	27,132	401.0	25.54	1.5	398.0	9,194	65.41	2.3
1956	30,585	463.3	28.81	1.5	419.2	9,905	58.64	2.4
1957	31,909	490.6	29.54	1.5	441.1	10,311	59.95	2.3
1958	32,894	517.0	30.27	1.6	447.3	10,302	58.91	2.3
1959	34,915	555.8	31.79	1.6	483.6	11,117	62.51	2.3
1960	36,287	584.1	32.69	1.6	503.8	11,932	66.04	2.4
1961	37,471	600.8	32.94	1.6	520.1	11,845	64.46	2.3
1962	40,575	631.6	34.01	1.6	560.3	12,381	66.33	2.2
1963	43,424	659.9	34.93	1.5	590.5	13,107	69.20	2.2
1964	47,403	700.7	36.43	1.5	631.7	14,155	73.67	2.2
1965†	51,996	760.6	38.87	1.5	681.2	15,120	77.71	2.2
1966†	57,500	821.0	41.22	1.4	740.0	16,500	83.94	2.2
Percentage Increases								
1946-1951	78.6	100.4	75.8	—	57.5	91.0	75.1	—
1951-1956	44.5	76.6	53.9	—	27.6	54.1	41.3	—
1956-1961	22.5	29.7	14.3	—	24.1	19.6	9.9	—
1961-1966	53.5	36.7	25.1	—	42.3	39.3	30.2	—
1946-1966	385.2	527.2	287.1	—	254.9	390.4	254.1	—

* Includes advertising commissions.
† Preliminary estimates.
Source: CANADA—Gross National Product figures for 1946-1965 from
National Accounts, Income and Expenditure, 1965, Dominion Bureau of

(Footnote continued on next page)

items as television sets and more sophisticated types of electrical appliances, as well as increasing competition among domestic manufacturers and distributors, and between Canadian suppliers and importers vying for the consumer dollar.

Following these two five-year periods of rapid growth, the rate of increase in advertising expenditures slowed down considerably in the next five-year period, 1956-1961, in line with the general slow-down of the economy as a whole. During this period advertising expenditures rose only by about 30 per cent, or less than one-half the rate of the 1951-1956 period, or one-third the rate of the 1946-1951 period.

The uncertainties in the economic outlook, a slowing-down in bringing new products to the market, a reduction in capital spending and increasing competition from suppliers of non-brand name products who relied much less on advertising than did brand-name product producers and distributors, all contributed to this reduction in the rate of growth in advertising expenditures in Canada during the 1956-1961 period.

In the more recent five-year period, 1961-1966, advertising expenditures rose slightly more rapidly, 37 per cent, than in

Statistics, Ottawa, 1966; and earlier issues; population statistics 1946-1966 from *Estimated Population of Canada, by Province at June 1, 1966,* Dominion Bureau of Statistics, Ottawa, 1966, and earlier issues; advertising expenditures are from the *Report* of the Royal Commission on Publications, Queen's Printer, Ottawa, 1961; from *Printing and Publishing Industry,* 1964, and *Radio and Television Broadcasting,* 1964, Dominion Bureau of Statistics, Ottawa, 1966 and earlier issues; and supplementary estimates from MacLean-Hunter Research Bureau, *A Report on Advertising Revenues in Canada,* Toronto, October 1966; "Gross Ad Revenues Expected to Go Up", *Marketing,* November 25, 1966, p. 79. UNITED STATES—Gross National Product and population statistics for 1946-1965 are from *Economic Report of the President, January 1966,* and *Economic Indicators, December 1966,* prepared for the Joint Economic Committee by the Council of Economic Advisers, United States Government Printing Office, Washington, D.C., 1966; advertising expenditures 1946 to 1965 are from *Statistical Abstracts of the United States,* U.S. Department of Commerce, United States Government Printing Office, Washington, D.C., 1966; the 1966 estimate is from "The Strategy: Market for Growth", *Printers Ink,* January 13, 1967, p. 9; all other data are special estimates.

the preceding five-year period. But since costs of advertising rose significantly during this period—though the extent of such cost increases cannot be measured adequately in the absence of appropriate statistics—the increase in the *volume* of advertising over the 1961-1966 period appears to be somewhat less than in the 1956-1961 period.

This slow-down in the growth of advertising expenditures is even more remarkable since it took place at a period of rapid expansion of the economy as a whole. It raises important questions:

Are business firms gradually learning more about the marginal utility of additional advertising expenditures?[5] Are business firms finding it necessary to limit the expansion of their advertising budgets because of growing uncertainties about longer-term economic prospects? Are business firms turning increasingly to other means of sales promotion, with advertising being accorded a relatively lesser role in their sales efforts? Are business firms not fully satisfied with the effectiveness of their advertising campaigns and the results they obtain? Are business firms holding their advertising budgets within bounds to keep costs down?

Trends in the United States in the last five years suggest that business firms continue to rely heavily on advertising expenditures as a means of reaching the consumer on the widest possible scale. For example, total advertising expenditures in the United States rose by 39 per cent over the period 1961-1966, or double the rate over the preceding five-year period, 20 per cent (see Table 1). Why the difference?[6]

All these are questions that the users, as well as the suppliers, of advertising and their advisers (i.e. the advertising agencies) will wish to consider. Answers to these questions are essential

---

5 This refers to the recognition that there is a point at which additional advertising expenditures bring such a small additional net revenue as to make it not worthwhile for business firms to undertake them.

6 See Chapter 5.

if the advertising industry is to chart its course for the next decade on a planned rather than improvised basis.

Currently, gross advertising expenditures are placed at $821 million. Projections prepared in another study suggest that advertising expenditures may reach between $1.1 billion and $1.2 billion in 1970[7] and between $1.7 billion and $1.9 billion by 1975.[8]

The projections are based on the assumption that advertising expenditures may rise over the next decade at least at as rapid a rate as Gross National Product and possibly at a somewhat greater rate. Some of the reasons advanced in support of this assumption include:

1. new technological advances will create new wants leading to new ways in meeting these wants;
2. growing complexity and specialization of markets;
3. significant changes in selling and advertising techniques;
4. increased competition.[9]

Gross Advertising Expenditures Per Capita

Canada has a population of about 20 million people. With spending on advertising of about $821 million, this means an average annual outlay of $41 per person. This works out to about 11 cents per day.

If all advertising expenditures could be eliminated and if there were no other costs involved that would either in part or in full offset the reduction of advertising costs, then the most that could be saved would be 11 cents per person per day. But this would be an impractical suggestion which even the most ardent critics of advertising would hesitate to put forward.

---

7 An industry study places gross advertising for 1970 at $1,047 million (see "Gross Ad Revenues Expected to Go Up", *Marketing*, November 25, 1966, p. 79).
8 *Broadcast Advertising in Canada, Past and Future Growth, op. cit.*, p. 224.
9 *Ibid.*, p. 223.

There are many types of advertising that are essential to the function of the economic system and that Canadians continued to use even during World War II, the period of the greatest conservation of resources for civilian use in the history of this country.

Assuming for the moment that two-thirds of total advertising expenditures are essential to the operation of the economic system[10]—and this assumption would require a definition of essentiality and its test in the light of quantitative evidence obtainable—all that Canadians could save would be less than 4 cents per person per day.

If such a cut-back were considered desirable, it could be achieved for example by removing all commercials from radio and television stations and by reducing newspaper advertising by one-third. All private radio and television stations would have to close down and the Canadian taxpayer would have to be prepared to pay one-quarter of the operating costs of the C.B.C. which are presently covered through revenues from advertising. Canadian newspapers would be unable to continue to give their readers the service to which they have been accustomed in the past and which they expect in the future as part of twentieth century living. With the quality of American newspapers remaining unaffected, Canadians might be tempted to turn increasingly to this source of information. Since Canadians are accustomed to an alternative program service, they would be turning to a much greater extent to American channels and radio stations. And where they could not reach American channels directly, there would be great pressure to extend cable television to all areas of Canada further away from the border. The provision that 55 per cent of Canadian programs had to be indigenous would lose its practical meaning.

---

[10] Professor Taplin suggests that essential advertising in the United Kingdom may be of the order of 70 per cent, with the less essential type of advertising about 30 per cent—what he calls "the disputed proportion". (See *Advertising, A New Approach, op. cit.*, p. 126.)

Would this be acceptable to Canadians? The subject is discussed further on in Chapter 13 under the heading "Implications of a Cut in Advertising on Communication Media".

Gross Advertising Expenditures and Gross National Product

Currently, about 1.4 cents out of every dollar of goods and services produced goes to advertising. This ratio is based on the 1966 experience, with preliminary estimates suggesting gross advertising expenditures of about $821 million and a Gross National Product of about $57.5 billion.

The proportion of advertising expenditures to Gross National Product rose from 1.1 per cent in 1946 to 1.6 per cent in the 1958-1962 period. Since then the ratio has been declining slightly, to about 1.4 per cent in 1966 (see Table 1).

It is noteworthy that during the last six years when Canada was going through the most protracted expansion phase in her peacetime history, Gross National Product rose more rapidly than advertising expenditures. The increase amounted to 54 per cent for the Gross National Product and 37 per cent for advertising expenditures over the period 1961-1966.

Thus, the facts do not support the claim that advertising expenditures in aggregate have been a strong contributing factor to inflationary pressures in the more recent period. They have risen at a slower rate than Gross National Product, as well as such other important economic flows as personal disposable income, consumer spending and personal savings. (Supplementary evidence on this subject is examined in Chapter 14.)

Gross and Net Advertising Expenditures

Net advertising expenditures equal gross advertising expenditures less advertising agency commissions. For the first seven years after the end of World War II, advertising agency commissions represented about 6.6 per cent of total gross advertising expenditures. They moved up to 7 per cent in 1953, and then further to 7.4 per cent in the 1960-1962 period. Since then the ratio has been declining slightly, to about 7.2 per cent in 1966. This amounts to $55 million, based on the 1966 preliminary estimates (see above) of $821 million gross and $766 million net advertising expenditures.[11]

Since the ratio of advertising agency commissions to gross advertising expenditures has moved within a fairly narrow band of 0.4 per cent during the period 1953-1966, analysis of changes in trends of advertising expenditures can be done either in terms of gross or net figures, without affecting significantly the results obtainable.

National and Local
Advertising Expenditures

National advertising expenditures are made by large business firms promoting brand name products and those interested in enhancing their corporate image. Many of these firms are heavy users of broadcast advertising, particularly television.

Local advertising expenditures are made by large retail distributors and other small or medium sized business firms and individuals, and by national advertisers using local advertising as a supplementary means of attracting customers for brand name products. Probably the greatest spenders (in terms of dollars) of local advertising expenditures are the food chains and department stores. Eaton's and Simpson's use of the Toronto and Montreal newspapers is a good example. The rates at which they buy may be lower than those available to a national advertiser. A great part of local advertising goes to newspapers and to some extent to local radio stations.

Governments and institutions use either national or local advertising, depending on the purpose of the advertising. For example, when the Government of Canada advertises the sale

---

11 "Gross Ad Revenues Expected to Go Up", *op. cit.*, p. 79.

of saving bonds, it will do so on a national scale. If a university publishes a notice of its registration requirements and courses given, it will do so in a local newspaper.

In 1966, about 64½ per cent of total broadcast advertising came from national sales. In 1961, the proportion was 63 per cent. Hence local advertising which amounted to 37 per cent in 1961 declined somewhat in relative importance to 35½ per cent in 1966.

In the case of newspaper advertising, national advertising comprised 31 per cent in 1966 as compared with 32½ per cent in 1961. Local advertising in newspapers rose from 67½ per cent of the total in 1961 to 69 per cent in 1966.

Thus, a different pattern is emerging, with local advertising becoming relatively more important in the case of newspapers, while national advertising is becoming relatively more important in the case of broadcast media. These different trends are illustrated by the following data:[12]

	1961 ($ millions)	1966 ($ millions)	Percentage Increase 1961-1966
Broadcast Advertising			
National	65.4	117.5	79.7
Local	38.4	64.0	66.7
Total	103.8	181.5	74.8
Newspaper Advertising			
National	70.0	87.9	25.6
Local*	145.5	193.2	33.7
Total	215.5	281.1	30.4

* Includes "classified" advertising.

The reasons for the more rapid growth of local advertising expenditures in the case of newspapers, as compared with national advertising expenditures over the last five years, can be explained:

1. The increase in participation of national advertisers in local advertising, e.g. national manufacturers sharing in the ad-

---

12 *Ibid.*

vertising costs at the local distribution level. A sizable portion of this type of advertising involves what the industry describes as "co-op" dollars.

2. More rapid rate of increase of advertising rates for local advertising.

3. Increasing pressures to promote sales at the local level in such highly competitive areas as food sales by chains.

4. Growth of shopping centres leading to a struggle for survival between centre town business and department and specialty stores located close to the main residential areas.

5. More local advertising by public authorities.

The explanation of the relative increase in national advertising on broadcast media includes the growing reliance of major corporations on television advertising carried by the two networks, the C.B.C. and C.T.V., and their affiliated stations.

The data reflecting diverse trends with respect to the growth of national and local advertising expenditures going to different communication media counsel care in making any generalizations. Much more research work would be needed to establish to what extent and in what form advertising allowances[13] made available by national firms to regional or local distributors[14] introduce a bias into aggregate figures because they do not fully reflect the total impact of national firms in the advertising picture.

---

13 "The origin of advertising allowances seems to have been in the desire of manufacturers to secure promotion of their products at the point of sale and their willingness to make contributions toward the expenses that dealers might incur in advertising their products. In recent years, the term 'advertising allowances' has been used to cover a wide variety of possible services. In fact it has often been a disguise for discounts or rebates in price. . . . Advertising allowances were found to be based directly on volume of purchases." (See *Discriminatory Pricing Practices in the Grocery Trade, op. cit.,* p. 205.)

14 The bulk of advertising allowances goes to chain stores.

Advertising Expenditures
Going to Different Media

The following tabulation shows the relative importance of the distribution of net advertising expenditures for major groups of communication media for the years 1961 and 1966:[15]

	1961		1966*	
	Amount ($ millions)	Percentage	Amount ($ millions)	Percentage
Radio	49.8	8.9	79.5	10.4
Television	54.1	9.7	102.0	13.3
Total Broadcasting	103.9	18.6	181.5	23.7
Newspapers	215.5	38.5	281.1	36.8
Periodicals	83.2	14.9	100.5	13.1
Other Printed Media	118.6	21.2	152.0	19.8
Total Printed Media	417.3	74.6	533.6	69.7
Other	38.3	6.8	50.5	6.6
Total	559.5	100.0	765.6	100.0

* Preliminary estimates.

What the data suggest is that the broadcasting media, particularly television, have been the most rapidly growing outlets for advertising in Canada in recent years, especially since the opening of new private television stations in major metropolitan cities in Canada in the early 1960's.

In the more recent period, indications have appeared that revenues received by broadcasting media have been rising at a reduced rate of growth. But in looking at developments over the last decade and a half, it appears that notwithstanding the more rapid increase in advertising expenditures going to broadcasting stations, all advertising media have made progress. In the case of broadcasting, the progress is particularly substantial in percentage terms because of the introduction of a new medium— television being introduced into Canada in 1952. But in absolute

---

[15] *Broadcast Advertising in Canada, Past and Future Growth, op. cit.,* p. 46, and "Gross Ad Revenues Expected to Go Up", *op. cit.,* p. 79.

terms, newspaper advertising has made the greatest gains as the
summary tabulation below suggests:[16]

	Increases: 1950-1965	
	Absolute Amounts ($ millions)	Percentage
Broadcast Advertising	136	565
Newspapers	156	167
Periodicals	58	171
Other Printed Media	74	122
Outdoor Advertising	42	561
Total Advertising	466	212

Ratios of Advertising Expenditures to Sales

How much does Canadian business spend on advertising in relation to sales? The scantiness of available data is illustrated by
the fact that the last official survey on the subject undertaken by
the Dominion Bureau of Statistics is twelve years old. Figures are
available on the ratio of advertising expenditures to sales for
manufacturing, wholesale and retail trades and certain services
for the year 1954.[17]

Since this was the first survey of its kind, certain definitional
and coverage problems were encountered which limit the usefulness of the data. Using the figures solely for the purpose of illustration rather than measurement, the main indications are these:

1. The ratio of advertising expenditures to sales is much
higher for goods than for services. For example, the highest
ratio for manufactured products was for toilet preparations, 15.9
per cent, while the highest ratio for the service sector applied to
theatres, 8.1 per cent.

2. Within the commodity sector, there are great variations
in the ratio, with a few items involving ratios of between 11 and
16 per cent including toilet preparations, breakfast foods and
soap and washing compounds. But the majority of items have

---

16 *Broadcast Advertising in Canada, Past and Future Growth, op. cit.*,
     p. 46.
17 *Advertising Expenditures in Canada, 1954.* Dominion Bureau of Statis-
     tics, Reference Paper No. 67, Queen's Printer, Ottawa, 1956.

ratios of between 1 and 2 per cent, with a considerable number of items showing ratios below 1 per cent.

3. The ratio was comparatively low for most essential items required for everyday living. Higher ratios applied mainly to special foods, certain household items and cosmetics. Low ratios included such basic items as food and beverages, 1.6 per cent; motor cars, 1.4 per cent; bread and bakery products, 1.3 per cent; and children's clothing (factory), 0.2 per cent.

4. In the retail trade, the ratio was higher for chain stores than for independent stores, with some of the leading retail groups showing the following ratios: jewellery stores, 3.7 per cent; furniture stores, 3.5 per cent; men's clothing stores, 3.2 per cent; women's clothing stores, 1.5 per cent. In contrast with these stores, other retail outlets showed much lower ratios: independent fruit and vegetable stores, 0.1 per cent; confectionery, tobacco stores and meat markets, each 0.2 per cent.

5. The average ratio for the manufacturing sector as a whole was given as 1.7 per cent. This proportion is close to the ratio for all industries, if the latter is measured in terms of the proportion of gross advertising expenditures to Gross National Product which amounted to 1.5 per cent in 1954 (see Table 1).

More adequate data available over a period of time would assist greatly in offering some more specific comments. In the absence of such information all that can be said is that most industries provide the consuming public with essential products and services required for everyday living by spending less on advertising in relation to the sales dollar than is the case in selling goods and services which provide consumers with the comforts and luxuries of life.

This observation is based on 1954 data. It assumes that there has not been a basic change in the practice of Canadian business firms to be more economical with advertising in relation to the sales dollar. Some changes, however, are likely to have occurred in a few industries. An example would be the drug industry. In this industry the advertising to sales ratio was a little over 6 per cent in 1954. The proportion may be higher in the 1960's if one is permitted to generalize from the evidence on promotional and advertising costs of drugs distributed in Canada, as submitted to the Royal Commission on Health Services.[18]

The key point, assuming general applicability of the figures published by the Dominion Bureau of Statistics twelve years ago, is that the low ratio of advertising expenditures to sales for most basic necessities of life, such as 1.6 per cent for food and beverages, 1.4 per cent for motor cars, and 1.9 per cent for electrical equipment, leaves little room for any significant reduction in prices by eliminating advertising expenditures—quite apart from the fact that such an elimination of advertising expenditures or a substantial reduction would lead to disruption of business practice with likely increases in costs and prices.

Growth Implications

The Canadian advertising industry is a growth industry. It has shown greater stability than many other industries and it has contributed to national economic stability, a point developed further in Chapter 6. Still, in the period of Canada's most rapid and protracted expansion phase, 1961-1966, advertising expenditures have not kept pace with the growth of the economy as a whole.

The question arises: Why?

Again, in the absence of a study in depth, only a few generalizations can be offered—and these are tentative, subject to review in the light of new evidence becoming available.

1. Increases in advertising expenditures are affected by the marginal utility of advertising. There is a point in increasing advertising expenditures where an additional amount spent will produce a return in terms of increased sales and profits which businessmen will consider insufficient to justify spending further

---

18 *Report* of the Royal Commission on Health Services, Queen's Printer, Ottawa, 1964, Chapters 16 and 17.

sums on advertising. That point will differ from industry to industry, firm to firm, commodity to commodity, and from medium to medium.

Even though in the present state of progress in the social sciences marginal utility of advertising expenditures has not been measured on an industry or an aggregative basis, it is a factor that may contribute to a slowing down in the rate of increase in advertising expenditures, particularly at a time when the economy as a whole is expanding rapidly.

2. National corporations seem to have been slowing down the rate of increase in their advertising budgets, as far as amounts which they spend directly are concerned. Against this there appears to have been some increase in advertising allowances to distributors, partly because of the increasing importance of "big" buyers, the chain and department stores, and partly because of increasing competition, both among the brand-name product producers, and between brand-name product producers and private brand product suppliers (see Chapter 9).

3. The spill-over effect of American advertising has meant that, to the extent that products sold in Canada are handled by subsidiaries of American corporations or by Canadian distributors representing U.S. firms, such products are marketed to some extent on the basis of advertising in American periodicals and on American broadcasting stations to which Canadians have access, both because they read these publications or because they watch television on U.S. channels and listen to American radio stations.

There does not exist in Canada a measurement of the spill-over effect of American advertising into Canada. But the fact that Canadian advertising expenditures have been rising at a slower rate in the last five years than advertising expenditures in the United States, even though the Canadian economy expanded more rapidly than the U.S. economy, is suggestive of the possibility that the spill-over effect of American advertising on the Canadian economy is greater than is either known or admitted in Canada (see Chapter 5).

5

Comparison

Advertising — Canada and United States

Canadians spend on an average about $41 per person on advertising a year, or less than one half of what Americans spend, about $84 (see Table 1). This difference has changed remarkably little over the last twenty years, though there were periods when advertising expenditures rose more rapidly in Canada than in the United States, thus narrowing somewhat the wide gap that exists in advertising expenditures per capita between the two countries.

Right after World War II, the ratio of advertising expenditures per capita as between Canada and the United States was 45 per cent, with the Canadian spending amounting to $10.65 and American spending to $23.70. Between 1946 and 1951, advertising expenditures per capita in Canada and in the United States rose at similar rates, about 75 per cent. In the next two five-year periods, 1951-1956 and 1956-1961, the rate of increase was somewhat more rapid in Canada than in the United States—54 per cent and 14 per cent respectively as compared with 41 per cent and 10 per cent respectively.

But the situation has been reversed in the last five years. During 1961-1966 advertising expenditures per capita in the

United States appeared to have risen more rapidly than in Canada—30 per cent as compared to 25 per cent (see Table 1).

Over the last twenty years, advertising expenditures per capita in Canada rose by 287 per cent and in the United States by 254 per cent. In 1966, advertising expenditures in Canada estimated at 41.22[1] are equivalent to about 49 per cent of the corresponding U.S. figure 83.94.[1]

While the percentage increases in per capita figures as between the two countries are roughly of a similar general order, with the rate of increase in Canada slightly ahead of the U.S. rate, in terms of total amounts spent on advertising Canadian expenditures have risen much more rapidly over the last two decades than U.S. expenditures. The increases for the two countries are 527 per cent and 390 per cent respectively. But the increase in total expenditures has been largely due to the more rapid growth of Canada's population. Very little of the increase has been due to a narrowing of the differences that exist in advertising spending in Canada as compared with such spending on a per capita basis in the United States.

The question arises: Why do Canadians spend a little less than one half of what Americans spend on advertising on a per capita basis? What are the reasons for this difference and why has there been so little change over the last two decades?

Reasons for Differences

In considering possible explanations of the reasons for the differences that exist in advertising expenditures per capita as between Canada and the United States, two points should be borne in mind.

The first (and this point bears repeating) is that more research and investigation is needed to obtain an adequate insight into the reasons for such differences as are indicated by broad overall aggregative figures. For totals sometimes hide more than

---

1 Preliminary estimates.

they reveal and there is need to consider the basic causes that yield the aggregate figures summarized in Table 1.

The other point is the difference in size between the Canadian and American economies. The U.S. population is currently ten times that of Canada. Gross National Product is about thirteen times that of Canada. Advertising expenditures are over twenty times those of Canada.[2]

Another study offers some preliminary answers as to possible reasons for the differences in advertising expenditures per capita in Canada as compared to those in the United States. Five reasons are given:

1. The U.S. industry caters to a domestic market 13 times the size of the Canadian market, representing the largest single market in the world in both absolute and per capita terms. To take full advantage of the economies of scale that can be obtained in catering to such a huge market, industry must exert intensive efforts to sell the goods and services it is capable of producing. To achieve this, greater advertising expenditures per capita and per dollar of sale are required than is the case in Canada where the market is much smaller.

2. The bulk of the advertising in the United States is done by national advertisers representing large corporations with a great stake in the production, distribution and financial sectors. Most of these large corporations take a long-term point of view about the potential benefits to be derived from advertising and they spend on advertising a considerably greater proportion of their sales budget than do many of the smaller Canadian companies.

3. The American consumer is advertising prone. He is receptive to new ideas and to new products. He is willing to consider

---

2 There are some differences in the quality of the estimates and in the coverage of advertising expenditures in the two countries. But such differences do not appear to be substantial enough to invalidate an assessment in general terms of the relative importance of advertising expenditures in Canada and the United States.

trying out new goods and new services if these are presented to him in an attractive and persuasive manner. The Canadian consumer is more conservative. He is likely to follow the lead of the American consumer once new products have found acceptance in the United States. Larger advertising expenditures per capita in the United States than in Canada take account of the variations in consumer attitudes that exist between the two countries.

4. A certain amount of advertising in the United States, placed with U.S. media, influences Canadian consumers. This is the case because Canadians read most of the American magazines from *Life* to *Scientific American*. Hence, the Canadian reading public is exposed to advertising placed in American magazines selling American products in Canada, with such products being either produced by American subsidiaries operating in Canada or imported from the U.S. Similarly, advertising is placed with American radio and television stations that are tuned in by Canadians living near the American border, and this appears to cover the majority of Canadian citizens. Thus, some advertising expenditures placed in the U.S. create an impact on Canadian consumers, making it unnecessary for such companies to place advertising in Canadian media to the extent they might otherwise have done. This "spill-over" effect of advertising expenditures made in the U.S. is a contributing factor to advertising expenditures in Canada being lower on a per capita basis than in the U.S.[3]

5. Advertising costs per thousand potential customers reached are claimed by the advertising industry to be higher in the U.S. than in Canada. One of the reasons advanced is the much greater fragmentation of advertising media in the United States. Where the U.S. is served by a number of women's magazines, Canada has only one. In the television field, most Canadian major cities are served by two networks; in the United States, by three networks. Canadian television stations in the large

---

[3] Some international advertisers do charge off their Canadian subsidiaries with "overflow" advertising expense, thereby reducing the available advertising budget dollars to be spent in Canada.

urban centres in this country do not exceed two English language and one French language (in some cities only), while U.S. stations number as many as seven or more in major cities like New York and Chicago. There is, however, this offsetting factor as far as advertisers are concerned: the potential customer reached by U.S. advertisers with higher cost per thousand is a more affluent customer than his Canadian counterpart,[4] so that higher advertising expenditures are more than recouped by greater sales.[5]

Reasons for Lag

Having explained what some of the reasons for the differences may be for advertising expenditures per capita as between Canada and the United States, the next question is: Why has this difference not been narrowed notably, say over the last twenty years?

In 1946, for every dollar spent on advertising in the United States on a per capita basis, 45 cents were spent in Canada. In 1966, this proportion had risen slightly to 49 cents.

What particular factors are contributing to this slow change in the gap in advertising expenditures per capita as between Canada and the United States? Why has this gap not been narrowed more significantly, particularly in the light of Canadian endeavours to reduce the income differentials between the two countries, with earnings in a number of occupations in Canada having moved closer to American levels, though substantial differences still exist? And with income rising rapidly, one could suppose that business firms may have wished to try to obtain a greater share of the consumer dollar.

---

4 In 1964, personal income per capita in the United States amounted to $2,248 (U.S. dollars) and in Canada to $1,643 (Canadian dollars). Broadly speaking, this meant that for every dollar earned by an American worker, the average Canadian earned 73¢. (See *Second Annual Review*, Economic Council of Canada, Queen's Printer, Ottawa, December 1965, p. 53.)

5 *Broadcast Advertising in Canada, Past and Future Growth, op. cit.*, pp. 35-37.

There is a further factor that Canada is a bilingual country. Producing advertising in two languages adds to costs. Hence, on a cost basis, one could expect a somewhat smaller differential in advertising spending on a per capita basis between Canada and the United States than in fact exists. But this is apparently not the case, if the broad aggregative figures of advertising trends, referred to above, are indicative of the true situation.

The question is: Why?

A general answer is offered below in the hope that this subject may lead to further enquiry, elaboration and explanation of what appears to be a rather complex and interrelated phenomenon.

There seems to exist a *lag* in advertising efforts between Canada and the United States. The lag may be of three kinds: 1. An Innovation Lag; 2. A Psychological Lag; and 3. An Expenditure Lag.

1. *Innovation Lag.* American entrepreneurs are great product innovators and they bring continuously new and improved products to the market. Canadian businessmen usually follow the American lead—with a time lag. In most instances they wait until the new commodities have found a measure of consumer acceptance in the United States. Thus risk is reduced in Canada, as well as the need to spend relatively as much on advertising to achieve consumer acceptance in Canada as is being spent in United States. The reasons for this are twofold:

(a) Once a commodity has achieved consumer acceptance, less advertising may be necessary than during the build-up period of consumer demand—though increased advertising may be required subsequently in the light of changing competitive conditions and varying demand conditions.

(b) There is a spill-over effect of American advertising into Canada since Canadians have direct access to American broadcasting stations and they read American newspapers and periodicals.

The effect of innovations on investment and advertising, both in Canada and in the United States, is discussed further in Chapter 10.

2. *Psychological Lag.* In making decisions about additional capital expenditures, new product or resources development, marketing programs and advertising campaigns, businessmen take into account not only the sales and profit prospects as they affect their own operations. They also consider—and this applies particularly to major corporations—the state of the economy generally, government economic policies and the political, economic, social and international climate in which they operate.

Thus, in the current circumstances, decisions of management of large business corporations are made in a *total* environment, as distinct from the decision-making process of earlier decades when government policy and international factors played a much lesser role in affecting the course of business than they do today.

Most of the time, entrepreneurs in the United States are imbued with a psychology of optimism and positiveness which has no parallel in the world. This characteristic of American management has been a major driving force in building up the U.S. economy to a level of wealth and productiveness unmatched in any other country.

Rising wealth in turn has created, as Professor Johnson put it, "a steady widening of the available range of choice, and the necessity of decisions about how the increasing capacity for choice is to be utilized".[6]

American businessmen have learned a great deal about the motivation and the attitudes of their buying public and they have formulated what they consider the most effective ways of meeting the growing needs of an increasingly affluent society, bent not only on having more money, more goods and services and more leisure, but also a greater choice in the manner in which their wants can be met, and a greater opportunity to

---

6 *The Canadian Quandary, op. cit.,* p. 270.

experiment with different ways of maximizing human satisfaction, both in material and non-material terms.

This is precisely the climate conducive to leadership—in business, in labour, in the professions and in government. Business psychology, which draws its strength from consumer psychology, is likely to undertake under all but the most discouraging circumstances—e.g. a serious recession—new ventures, seeking out new opportunities and creating them when necessary.

While Canadian management has a high regard for American initiative and enterprise, it prefers in most instances to follow American leadership. This attitude is quite understandable because most Canadian corporations are smaller in size than American business firms. Since Canadian companies have lesser financial resources at their disposal than their American counterparts, they cannot take the risk or underwrite the development costs that are involved in launching major new commodities, on the scale that American firms do.

Hence the psychological lag that appears to exist between Canadian and American management in proceeding with new developments—which in turn may be accompanied by increased advertising efforts—can be explained in part by the existence of great differentials in wealth, levels of income and size of markets. In part it may be due to differences in cultural and traditional attitudes which characterize the Canadian and American people.

But whatever the explanation, a psychological lag appears to exist between the two countries, and this would affect business decisions in general, as well as decisions to formulate advertising campaigns.

3. *Expenditure Lag.* Given the differences in the rate of timing at which innovations are introduced in Canada and the United States, and allowing further for the differences in business psychology, with American entrepreneurs being more venturesome and Canadian entrepreneurs being more conservative,

it follows that there would be differences in business investment which in turn would affect changes in the level of advertising expenditures.

The fact that advertising expenditures rose more rapidly in the United States in the 1961-1966 period, should not, however, be taken as an indication that Canadian advertising expenditures would of necessity continue to lag behind the United States. The essence of the lag is that it works in two directions: Canada may be behind the rate of increase in advertising expenditures in the United States in one period; but in a subsequent period, when the rate of increase in the United States may be slowing down, Canadian advertising expenditures may continue at a rate of increase of an earlier period, which may now exceed that of the United States. Sooner or later the Canadian rate may follow the downward trend of the American rate—again with a time lag.

In summary, then, there are a number of reasons why Canada may continue to spend less on advertising on a per capita basis than the United States. Some progress may be made toward narrowing the gap that exists at present, but the experience of the last twenty years suggests that such progress is likely to be slow.

What could contribute to a possible speed-up in the effort to narrow the gap in per capita advertising expenditures between Canada and the United States would be the endeavour on the part of Canadian advertisers, advertising agencies and advertising media to learn more about making more effective use of the $821 million currently spent on advertising. This represents a particularly important objective since there exists the possibility that advertising expenditures in Canada may double over the next decade. Only adequate study, planning and leadership will make it possible for the advertising industry to reach this objective and to ensure that the advertising dollars spent produce the best results for their clients.

6

Stability

The critics of advertising hold that one of its disadvantages is that it contributes to economic instability. To illustrate:

> Advertising expenditures tend to move with, and so contribute to, the business cycle: one can indeed trace the business cycle by the varying thickness of newspapers and magazines from year to year, which reflects the amount of advertising revenue.[1]

Other economists make more qualified observations. Professor Borden, for example, emphasizes that advertising is not likely to be a significant factor in contributing to cyclical changes in economic activity. To quote:

> Advertising cannot be classed as an important causal factor in cyclical fluctuations, although the way in which businessmen have used advertising leads to the conclusion that it has tended to aggravate cyclical fluctuations. None of the students of cyclical fluctuation have named advertising as an important causal factor. Moreover, fluctuations occurred before advertising became an important factor in the economy.[2]

Professor Borden's analysis is largely based on the experience of four recession and depression periods in the United States,

---

[1] *The Canadian Quandary, op. cit.,* p. 293.
[2] *The Economic Effects of Advertising, op. cit.,* p. 273.

1907, 1914, 1920 and 1929 (and the years following). The evidence available for these periods appears to support Professor Borden's contention that advertising expenditures and general economic activity move up together in prosperous times and decline in periods of economic adversity.

However, evidence available for the post-World War II period, though not fully conclusive, suggests that the pattern may be changing somewhat. Whether the reason is greater sophistication on the part of advertisers, changes in the role of advertising in economic affairs, greater effectiveness of such new mass media as television, or some other reason, is not clear.

Canada, like the United States, went through four periods of recession since the end of World War II. In all four recessions, advertising expenditures in Canada increased. Gross National Product continued to rise through three periods of recession and only declined during the 1953-1954 recession, but even in that year, the decline was so moderate as to be tantamount to a levelling off of the Gross National Product.[3]

Advertising expenditures in Canada rose through the four recessions as follows: 1948-1949 by 15 per cent, 1953-1954 by 10 per cent, 1957-1958 by 5 per cent and 1960-1961 by 3 per cent.

In the United States, advertising expenditures rose during the 1948-1949 recession and during the 1953-1954 recession, 7 per cent and 5 per cent respectively (see Table 1). In the 1957-1958 recession, advertising expenditures levelled off and in the 1960-1961 recession, they declined by less than 1 per cent.

This analysis is based on officially published data of advertising expenditures.[4] New estimates prepared as a result of private

[3] This analysis is based on annual data. The decline is somewhat more apparent if quarterly data of Gross National Product, in constant dollars seasonally adjusted, are used.

[4] The officially published data are based largely on estimates prepared by the advertising industry itself. Professional advertisers familiar with the advertising expenditure statistics readily admit that the estimates are approximate and subject to substantial improvements (see also source notes to Table 1).

research efforts show continuing increases in advertising expenditures during the period 1947-1966. In the two periods which show a decrease and a levelling off in advertising expenditures in the United States in the officially published statistics, the newly developed data show increases during the two recessionary periods: 1957-1958, a rise from $10,313 million to $10,414 million (new data) as against a levelling off, $10,311 million and $10,302 million respectively (officially published data); 1960-1961, a rise from $11,900 million to $12,048 million (new data) as against a decrease, $11,932 million and $11,845 million respectively (officially published data).[5]

The four recessions experienced in Canada and in the United States during the postwar period have generally been shorter and less in extent than economic fluctuations experienced in North America in the 1920's and 1930's. While the economic impact of advertising on sales cannot be isolated because of the interrelationship that exists with many other factors contributing to variations in sales volume, the fact remains that the economies of Canada and the United States have been subjected to less severe economic fluctuations in the post-World War II period, and advertising expenditures have generally been rising on an annual basis as businessmen endeavoured to obtain their share of expanding markets in times of prosperity and to bolster declining sales in periods of recession.[6]

The observations offered above do not tie in with another study made in the United States. This study, using quarterly data of national advertising expenditures in the United States, suggests that there is a closer relationship between variations in advertising spending and fluctuations in general economic activity than is indicated in annual data. To quote:

---

[5] The new data were developed by Charles Y. Yang, in collaboration with Seymour Banks and Richard W. Strain (see "Economy Soars, U.S. Advertising Volume Rises 8% to $16.8 Billion in 1966, AA's Yang Estimates Show", by Charles Y. Yang, Seymour Banks and Richard W. Strain, *Advertising Age*, December 19, 1966, p. 54.)

[6] *Broadcast Advertising in Canada, Past and Future Growth, op. cit.,* p. 39.

In the postwar period, national advertising, as best we can measure it, has fully conformed to the pattern of general business activity. There is no evidence of major counter-cyclical activity, nor has national advertising skipped any peaks or troughs in general business. Nor has national advertising varied within cycles of its own timing, as are found in, say, the textile industry or even automobiles. . . . While national advertising conforms closely to the business cycle, it does not conform precisely. Peaks in advertising tend to lag somewhat behind the peaks in general business.[7]

The American study, referred to above, covers national advertising expenditures rather than total advertising expenditures. But whether annual or quarterly data are used, they are still inadequate for the purpose of cyclical analysis for which monthly data are required.

Another study based on quarterly and annual data, comparing cyclical behaviour of national advertising on eight major media with changes in the Gross National Product and the Industrial Production Index, comes to a similar conclusion: a fairly close correlation between changes in economic activity and the amounts spent by business on national advertising in the post-World War II period, continuing the pattern of earlier periods in American economic history. To quote:

Our analyses of the cyclical behavior of individual national advertising media reveal that advertising in general has been highly responsive to fluctuations in general business activity during the postwar period. Yet, the degree of such responsiveness and the pattern of fluctuations vary from medium to medium, depending on the nature of the medium and the economic climate surrounding it.

With only one exception, all media responded positively to the fluctuations in gross national product and industrial production during the four postwar contraction and three expansion periods. The only exception was observed in 1954 when tele-

---

7 "Forecasting National Advertising Volume", by David M. Blank, in *How Business Economists Forecast*, edited by William F. Butler and Robert A. Kavesh, Prentice-Hall Inc., Englewood Cliffs, New Jersey, 1966, p. 387.

vision network advertising escaped the impact of recession by responding adversely to a decline in general business activity.[8]

The author offers the following conclusions: "Our examination of annual data indicates that advertising has been quite responsive to fluctuations in the economy, although the degree of such responsivness varies somewhat from one medium to another. It also reveals that advertising has become *more sensitive* to business cycles in recent years."[9]

Again this study bases its conclusions on national advertising expenditures rather than on total advertising expenditures. Estimates prepared by the same author some four years later show that total advertising expenditures going to all media have been rising in every year during the period 1946-1966.[10] One could have expected that some reduction in advertising expenditures may have occurred during the postwar period in response to declines of business activity during the four recessionary periods that occurred during the last two decades. But the annual data do not show such declines.

It is true that advertising expenditures have risen at varying rates. While some business firms may have reduced advertising expenditures for short periods of time or kept temporarily their spending at an unchanged level, there were other firms and institutions that kept raising their advertising expenditures during periods of recession. As a result, in each of the twenty years since the conclusion of World War II, total advertising expenditures, if the new estimates developed are to be believed, have involved greater amounts than in the year previous. Why?

Studies of advertising motivation and expenditures made by business and other sectors have not been pursued in sufficient depth and with adequate data to answer the question as to how

---

[8] "Study Shows How Advertising Lags Behind Business Cycles; 'Real' Ad Output Up Only 35% Since '20s Says Author", by Charles Yang, *Advertising Age*, October 15, 1962, p. 112.

[9] *Ibid.*, p. 114.

[10] "Economy Soars, U.S. Advertising Volume Rises 8% to $16.8 Billion in 1966, AA's Yang Estimates Show", *op. cit.*, p. 54.

changes in business prospects do in fact affect advertising expenditures and why total advertising expenditures in the United
States and in Canada have continued to increase from year to
year, four recessions during the last twenty years notwithstanding.[11]

Here is another area where further research in Canada, as
in the United States, could provide a more definite answer to the
question: Does advertising, in the light of its changing role in
economic life, continue to contribute to cyclical variations, as it
did in earlier years, or is there a different pattern in the making?

---

[11] On the basis of the new estimates of total advertising expenditures
in the United States as developed by Charles Y. Yang (*Ibid.*).

7

Productivity

Types of Advertising Productivity

When reference is made to productivity in advertising, two aspects are involved. One is the productivity of the advertising process, and this refers to the effectiveness of advertising in inducing potential sales. The other is productivity of the operations of the advertiser as the result of, or at least in part induced by, the advertising process. The latter in turn may involve productivity increases in production or in distribution. What is involved in this instance is an attempt to ascertain to what extent, if any, advertising makes it possible for management to achieve economies in production and distribution.

Productivity of the Advertising Process

An assessment of the productivity of the advertising process involves measurement of the economic impact of advertising in relation to its costs. The objective is to ascertain whether a dollar spent on advertising in a newspaper, in a magazine, on radio or on television yields better results to the advertiser, that is sales of his products, than other promotional activities. But since sales are the result of many factors, including personal sales and promotional campaigns, neither business firms nor their advisers, the advertising agencies, have been able to establish quantitatively how much a given amount of advertising expenditure will yield in terms of sales, making the distinction between commodities and different media.

Similarly, difficulties are encountered in establishing scientifically the point at which marginal returns on advertising make further advertising expenditures uneconomical.

In practice, business firms have resorted to oversimplified measurements to relate costs to the results from advertising (see below). Further, business firms have endeavoured to determine the point at which advertising becomes unprofitable by experimentation and trial and error.

There are exceptions to the point that it is difficult to measure the effects of advertising on sales. This can be done in some areas of advertising, as for example when using mail-order catalogues, or other types of sales soliciting by mail. The greatest amount of work done on measuring the effects of advertising on sales has been by users of coupons in print ads. International Correspondence Schools are the foremost example. In such cases, it is possible to establish a direct relationship between the amount of sales and the promotional effort involved.

But such areas of direct measurement are limited. For the bulk of advertising, business firms and the advertising profession use different techniques.

The method most commonly used is to relate the cost of advertising to the number of potential customers reached. In the case of newspapers and magazines, this involves the setting of advertising rates based on circulation, i.e. the number of readers of a particular publication, as certified by an independent research or survey organization acceptable both to advertisers and media alike.

In the case of radio and television advertising, the concept of "cost per thousand" is used.[1] This measurement may be defined as follows:

> 'Cost per thousand' is the amount paid for an advertising message divided by the number of individual homes (multiplied by 1,000) which actually, as proven by surveys, viewed television or listened to radio at a particular time period. The basis of cost per thousand is a minute commercial rate though the same principle also applies to other advertising time periods purchased.[2]

Broadcast station operators look at the productivity of the advertising medium in a different way as compared to the advertiser. The station operator—and this applies mainly to the privately owned stations—endeavours to establish advertising rates on a basis which enables him to recoup his operating costs and make a reasonable return on his investment.

But the buyer of advertising time on radio or television will judge the advertisement on the basis of the results he may be able to obtain—and this he judges on the basis of the audience actually exposed to his commercials. Thus the advertiser endeavours to establish what he considers an effective cost efficiency from the point of view of his advertising message meeting his particular needs to merchandise his product.

The "cost per thousand" method indicates to the broadcast station operator whether or not his pricing is out of line with that of his competitors. At the same time this method gives the advertiser a yard-stick—albeit a crude one—to judge the effectiveness of the advertising dollars he may be spending on broadcasting media, as against spending a like amount for other types of advertising or, for that matter, other sales or promotional efforts.

---

[1] There are further refinements possible in this type of measurement, such as "Reach, Frequency and Penetration" analysis. The methodology involved is explained in *Broadcast Advertising in Canada, Past and Future Growth, op. cit.*, pp. 118-122.

[2] *Ibid.*, p. 108.

Measurement and Research

Advertising is one of the many factors affecting sales. It is a function of measurement and research to establish the contribution advertising makes to achieve certain sales targets.

George Gallup, one of the most experienced professionals in measuring audience responses, calls advertising in today's highly competitive market "often the dominant variable in many product fields—especially those where product features and prices are comparable and leading brands are widely distributed."[3]

Many problems are involved in producing "effective" advertising. Reduced to simplest terms, they fall, according to George Gallup, into five categories:

1. What to say—what sales ideas to present to win new customers and hold old ones.
2. Where to say it—what media to use.
3. How to say it—how to present sales arguments in the most interesting and convincing manner.
4. How to relate the advertising to sales results—what proof of sales can be found?
5. How much to spend—at what point do added advertising dollars not pay their way?[4]

Mr. Gallup's firm, Gallup & Robinson, has dealt with such questions over the last eighteen years. The following comments are offered: "The amount of money spent by different advertisers for a page of space in a given magazine—or a minute of time on a given television program—is a constant. What they receive in return for their expenditure is a variable. And this variable can be shockingly large. It is not unusual to find one advertiser registering his sales message on ten times as many prospects

---

[3] "Measuring Advertising's Sales Effectiveness: The Problem and the Prognosis", by George Gallup, in *Marketing Research*, edited by Evelyn Konrad and Rod Erickson, American Management Association, New York, 1966, p. 146.

[4] *Ibid.*

as his competitor in the same issue of a magazine and in the same amount of space."[5]

In the early fifties, new survey techniques were developed based on what was called the "Impact idea". The procedures involved are described in these terms:

> If a reader or viewer is exposed to an advertisement or commercial under normal conditions where his processes of selectivity have free play—where he can accept or reject the advertising message—then the effectiveness, or impact, of that ad can be gauged by the ability of the respondent to play back the advertiser's message at a later date without re-exposure. This method involves a long interview in depth, the only aid to recall being the advertiser's name and product. The data obtained in this manner permit evaluation of the effectiveness of an ad in terms of both its ability to register the name of the advertiser and the degree to which it was able to communicate selling ideas and create conviction. By studying the content and execution of ads which have been successful and unsuccessful in terms of these criteria, analysts are able to distill out from these data those principles of communication which make for the most effective advertising.[6]

This type of measurement had a great deal of influence on the evolving pattern of advertising in the United States over the last decade and a half, with Canadian businessmen following the lead of their American colleagues. To illustrate: advertising in magazines emphasizing a news approach which produced "performance premiums of some twenty percent" about doubled in the United States in the period since 1952 while the "gimmicky" type of advertising dropped from about one-third of total advertising "to something less than five percent of all advertising" over approximately the same period.[7]

More recently, new techniques have been developed to assess more effectively audience reaction to advertising exposures. One such technique is described as the "Activation method". This

---

5 *Ibid.*
6 *Ibid.*, pp. 146 and 147.
7 *Ibid.*, p. 147.

method is based on the premise that people appear to know what makes them buy.

Studies undertaken by Gallup & Robinson indicate that "people can retrace the mental steps that led to a purchase and in doing this they can give the researcher useful evidence as to the part which advertising did or did not play. Obviously a large proportion of respondents will still report that they purchased brand X because of the recommendation of a neighbour, or they might reveal that when they went to the store the sales clerk told them it was a better product for less money. Importantly, however, in response to the Activation interview consumers give advertising due credit for the sale. In the case of the purchase of all brands not heretofore used, nearly half of all respondents report that they got the idea for buying from advertising.[8]

The Activation method assists advertisers, according to its originators, in the main in three ways. It makes it possible for an advertiser to:

Continuously observe the selling power of a given advertising campaign, so that a worn-out campaign can be replaced. The new campaign can be audited to determine if it is an efficient replacement.

Compare one against another the selling power of individual TV shows, so that the weaker properties can be culled out of the program lineup.

Continuously observe the effectiveness of competitive marketing tactics, so that only those tactics actually doing some damage need be countered.[9]

Mr. Gallup offers this conclusion: "Activation is not a cure-all. But enough progress has already been achieved to indicate that we are on the edge of a solution. The method is a workable one, and the data have, in recent years, pointed unerringly to

8 *Ibid.*, p. 150.
9 *Ibid.*, p. 151.

the advertising campaigns which have had outstanding records for moving goods."[10]

Notwithstanding the claims that are being made of the increasing usefulness of measurement surveys and research efforts to establish and test the effectiveness of advertising as a factor in sales determination, both Canadian and American investigations have raised some doubt about the accuracy of such audience measurement surveys. For example, Congressional Hearings in the United States about the meaningfulness of broadcast rating surveys led the Investigating Committee to the conclusion: "Broadcast ratings are known to be inaccurate as indexes of consumer program preferences."[11]

While more sophisticated broadcast measurement surveys have been developed in Canada, as in the United States in recent years, the Canadian Committee on Broadcasting, in reviewing the results from audience rating surveys, concluded in its 1965 Report:

> There is need for greater knowledge of the social and human effects of broadcasting, which must be based on research. We know much too little about the impact of television and radio programs on the audience as a whole, and on particular groups. Until now, audience research has been largely confined to determining the number of sets tuned in at a given time to a particular program—the so-called ratings system. This tells nothing about the intensity of attention given to a program or its continuing impact, and—even for the commercial purpose for which it is used—gives an incomplete picture of audience reaction. Some useful audience research has recently been done by the C.B.C., but it could be extended and made more generally available, certainly to the C.B.A. and perhaps to the public.[12]

---

10 *Ibid.*

11 See Hearings held by the U.S. Congress, House Committee on Interstate and Foreign Commerce, *Evaluation of Statistical Methods Used in Obtaining Broadcast Ratings*, H.R. No. 193, 87th Cong., 1st Sess. 7-8, 12, 20-36, 59-87, 1961.

12 *Report* of the Committee on Broadcasting, Queen's Printer, Ottawa, 1965, p. 99.

The Committee on Broadcasting made a further plea for more marketing research and new approaches to marketing research in the broadcasting field. It stated: "The chief object of market research in broadcasting should be to identify every audience large enough to justify the cost to its related market of making a broadcasting approach."[13]

The Chairman of the Board of Broadcast Governors has outlined some areas where research could yield substantial results in enabling advertisers to make more effective use of broadcasting as an advertising vehicle. To quote:

> First, there is evidence that a substantial part of the audience uses the commercial time segments to withdraw from the screen and to do other things. Is this deliberate withdrawal necessary? How much attention has been given to ways and means of introducing the commercial message so as to reduce withdrawals or to circumvent it?

> Second, it is clear that a large part of the audience can remain in front of the screen without any part of the commercial message registering. Half an hour later, or less, they could not tell you what they had seen or heard. How is this kind of escape possible? Can anything be done to correct it?

> Third, how far is it true that the people who constitute the audience merely accept advertising on sufferance, and place no reliance on it? What difference would it make if a serious effort were made to increase the credibility of advertising messages?

> Fourth, there is strong reason to believe that some part of the audience finds some part of the commercials positively offensive. How is this related to the general attitude to all advertising? Is it necessary to offend even some of the audience? If not, what are the more acceptable alternatives?[14]

---

13 *Ibid.*, p. 222.
14 "How the Media Can Be Made More Effective Advertising Vehicles", Address by Dr. Andrew Stewart, Chairman of the Board of Broadcast Governors, to the Association of Canadian Advertisers, Toronto, May 2, 1961, pp. 11 and 12.

Another study made a plea for private industry-government research to assess the effectiveness of broadcast advertising by saying:

> Measurement alone, as sophisticated as it may be, does not fully answer the questions occupying broadcasters and advertisers alike. Why is one commercial more effective than another? Why does one program appeal to people more than another? Who listens or views what program and why? How do people react to certain commercials and what are the concrete results? What is the public attitude toward the increasing volume of advertising and at what stage does advertising approach a saturation point? What special groups are interested in special products and how can these special groups best be reached in terms of exposure and costs? . . .

> Research, however, has much broader ramifications than just program and advertising research. There is the area of supply and demand analysis that requires considerably greater attention in the future than it has received in the past. Royal Commissions, parliamentary and special committees and government agencies have over the last four decades explored in depth many aspects of the supply side of providing broadcast advertising services to Canadians. But comparatively little attention has been given to the changing, and in fact, growing demand for such services. There is the further need to explore more fully and more effectively the impact of the Canadian broadcasting system on the economy as a whole and the individual, covering social, psychological and human relationships and responses of the individual to the broadcasting medium.[15]

There is another area of investigation that, if properly pursued, can yield substantial results, so its proponents claim, in increasing the productivity of advertising, and that is: pre-testing consumer response to advertising messages.

A study undertaken by the National Industrial Conference Board in New York offers this conclusion:

> The cost of preparing an advertisement is usually just a fraction of that of exposing it to the intended audience. And

---

[15] *Broadcast Advertising in Canada, Past and Future Growth, op. cit.,* pp. 316 and 317.

the cost of determining, in advance, whether or not an advertisement will do the job desired is generally even less. Yet many millions of dollars (which could have been invested in productive advertising) have failed to yield results. . . . Often, simple and inexpensive pretests can prevent such losses.[16]

There is no dearth of suggestions to undertake more research to assess the productivity and effectiveness of the advertising process, particularly in such spectacular mass communication media as television. But so far, progress in this direction in Canada has been limited by the lack of initiative and of funds to develop a comprehensive research program—on the part of advertisers, advertising agencies, advertising media and governments.

Productivity in Production

The proponents of advertising claim that there are two ways in which advertising contributes to increasing productivity in production. One is through increasing the scale of manufacturing operations by widening the market. The other is through its contribution of consumer acceptance of new or improved products which could be produced more economically than older products.

By encouraging businessmen to proceed with new capital spending in the expectation of reaching a given market with the aid of advertising, as well as other promotional and sales efforts, such advertising contributes to increasing productivity in an indirect manner—so it is claimed—i.e. through increased investment (see Chapter 10).

Professor Borden, however, has emphasized that available cost data do not permit us "to trace a clear causal relationship between decreased production costs and advertising."[17]

Professor Borden noted that while some "indirect effects in reducing production costs" as a result of advertising could be

---

16 *Pretesting Advertising*, by Harry D. Wolfe, James K. Brown, Stephen H. Greenberg and G. Clark Thompson, National Industrial Conference Board, New York, 1963.

17 "The Economic Effects of Advertising", *op. cit.*, p. 263.

observed, the situation appeared to vary a great deal as between different industries. To quote:

> In the study of specific industries, numerous instances were noted in which manufacturers employed advertising to help gain sales volume and in which the increase in size was attended by economies, which in varying degree offset advertising expenditures. In certain instances studied, advertising played a considerable part in building industry demand, and the economies gained through increased size of factories as industry demand grew were apparently greater than the promotional expenditures. Among products discussed at length, this condition evidently held in the early days of the cigarette industry and clearly in the case of mechanical refrigerators; less intensive study of numerous other industries indicates that the condition has frequently held true.
>
> Not all industries, however, have had to rely upon the stimulus of advertising to build a demand sufficient to support low-cost manufacturing operations. The sugar, shoe, and sheeting industries, for example, grew to large size without much influence from advertising in stimulating primary demand, although aggressive selling in other forms was used.
>
> Once industry demand has been established, it is possible for producers to seek a volume of sales large enough to permit low costs of manufacture without employment of a substantial amount of advertising. This generalization applies clearly to industries such as the sugar industry, which never has been a substantial user of advertising, but it applies as well to industries in which many producers are advertisers. Thus, not only do numerous sugar refineries attain low costs of production with little advertising, but the same is true of certain producers of cigarettes, mechanical refrigerators, dentifrices, and numerous other products, who are operating in industries which have relatively high average ratios of advertising costs.[18]

Productivity and Distribution

Two factors have contributed to advertising playing such an important role in the economic life of North America. One has been the growth of the mass media. The other has been the

---

[18] *Ibid.*, pp. 263 and 264.

economies introduced into the selling efforts. Professor Johnson observes:

> Part of the explanation of the rise of modern advertising can be found in the concurrent development of large-scale production and large-scale merchandising, whose economies can only be realized by a large and stable volume of sales. Advertising men are fond of claiming the credit for making it possible to realize the economies of large-scale production and distribution. . . . A more fundamental explanation . . . lies in the development of cheap media of mass communication, which have made it possible to address messages to large numbers of people simultaneously at a far lower cost per person addressed than the cost of person-to-person selling, and so have fostered both the substitution of advertising for personal selling and increased emphasis on selling as a branch of business activity.[19]

David M. Blank emphasized further the distribution economies achieved through mechanizing the marketing process. To quote:

> The growth of advertising in recent years has paralleled and facilitated a substantial reduction in the amount of retail sales effort per unit of retail sales. The decline in the personal sales function resulting from the growth in supermarkets, discount houses, vending machines, and self-service operations in general has resulted in considerable growth in efficiency in distribution, an economic sector that has traditionally lagged behind goods-producing industries in gains in productivity. This shift to self-service has been largely dependent on the development of product differentiation and the expansion in advertising, for they involve a continuously greater need on the part of manufacturers for direct selling of customers and, indeed, of dealers.[20]

Most critics of advertising will admit that advertising may have contributed to production and distribution economies. But in looking over the large number of almost identical products, both brand-name and private-name items that fill the shelves of supermarkets, department and chain-stores and discount-

---

19 *The Canadian Quandary, op. cit.*, pp. 271 and 272.
20 "A Note on the Golden Age of Advertising", by David M. Blank, *The Journal of Business of the University of Chicago*, January 1964, p. 38.

houses, the question has been raised, understandably, as to whether all this product duplication and differentiation is really necessary. And the related question raised was whether the large expenditures made on advertising to promote the sales of these products have not added unnecessarily to the production and distribution costs and thus have raised prices which consumers have to pay.

In essence, the question that has been raised is: Are the social *net* costs of advertising such that the Canadian public would be better off with a reduction in advertising expenditures, or with a decrease in the number of products of the same or similar use value, thus lessening somewhat the competitive efforts of brand-name product suppliers for product differentiation if the latter brings to the consumer no other advantage than a greater choice, and no significant differences in quality and price (see Chapter 8).

Is Advertising Wasteful?

The answer to the question "Is Advertising Wasteful?" given by the Institute of Canadian Advertising is: "Sometimes."

In explaining the reasons for this view, the Institute named as the number one factor the nature of the economy, structured around the profit-and-loss system, and operating under competitive conditions. The Institute explained:

> In such a climate, management makes constant war on waste, for waste contributes to higher costs. The manufacturer who spends money on advertising when he could choose more productive channels of business development is wasting his resources. In our experience, client management is on guard against waste in advertising just as vigorously and as constantly as it watches for waste in material supplies, in work processes, and waste in time and effort. Wasted dollars, whether they be in advertising or any other part of the productive process, represent a needless cost and indicate management inefficiency; and inefficient companies operate at a severe handicap in a competitive atmosphere. . . .

Because of the high investment expense required, manufacturers today spend many months on market research—testing new products, and checking on consumer reaction and preferences before getting ready for national distribution. Ideally, a manufacturer would then develop a product suited in quality, style and price to a certain section of the market, and would spend his advertising dollars describing his product to only those interested and in an immediate position to buy. But how can one pick the precise time when a precise individual has the time, money, and inclination to make a specific purchase? The cost of isolating such individuals may be totally uneconomic. Mass media in a sense are bound to be wasteful—only a small percentage of the readers of a newspaper will read a particular advertisement—but the expectation is that response from that percentage will more than justify the cost, and the cost itself may be far less than other methods of selecting potential customers. Waste in communication is a highly relative term.

In addition, there are waste factors within advertising itself. There is poor advertising, just as there is poor design, and obsolete machinery, and outdated work procedures. . . .

In addition to those advertising campaigns which are not soundly conceived, or are misdirected, a campaign may be wasteful because of too much advertising—or because of too little. Theoretically, one should stop advertising at the point at which another dollar invested will not bring in more than a dollar's worth of sales. This exact point is difficult indeed to determine. The effect of advertising is cumulative and most brand advertising is long range; meanwhile, at any point in time the economic outlook may alter, a competitor may introduce a superior product, or a new promotion, or a better advertising campaign, or cut prices, or component products may become unavailable or rise sharply in price—and such factors may change the whole complexion of the marketplace.[21]

This is frank talk indeed by experts in the advertising profession. Presumably it presents an attempt to put into realistic

---

21 *Proceedings* of the Special Joint Committee of the Senate and House of Commons on Consumer Credit (Prices), December 13, 1966, pp. 1999 and 2000.

perspective the working of a substantially market-oriented economy relying largely on individual initiative and on the price system.

From a social point of view the real question is not whether waste occurs or does not occur in advertising or through advertising. What matters is whether such waste as does occur could be reduced or minimized, or alternative ways found to provide the necessary services leading to a desired pattern of resource allocation, achieved in the most efficient manner practicable.

The answer to this question has so far been pragmatic rather than scientific. As long as mass communications offer the most economic way of reaching consumers and distributing billions of dollars' worth of goods and services each year, with a maximum of effectiveness and a minimum of dislocation, advertising will remain the favourite means of selling and promotion.

In this context "waste" and "productivity" of advertising become relative concepts. As long as the mix of minimizing the former and maximizing the latter meets the test of the market, advertising will continue to play the role of an economic lubricant keeping an industrial society operating in high gear. But if advertising fails this test—and the increasing shift on the part of certain sectors of the business community to the "gimmicky" type of promotional type of activities (see Chapter 1) illustrates this possibility—entrepreneurs will search for more productive and economic alternatives of selling techniques.

This involves constant soul-searching among advertisers and their professional advisers—whether they are making the most efficient use of their advertising budgets and how they can do better in the future.

In this process, the mass communication media are also becoming involved. For as the demands of advertisers and agencies become more sophisticated, media will have to do better than just offering space or time for sale. They will be expected to provide the type of communication services which will assist businessmen to reach their economic objectives.

The search for increasing advertising productivity—like the search for true wisdom—is as elusive as it is continuing.[22]

---

[22] See also Chapter 12 for a discussion of the ability of a wealthy society to afford some "waste".

8

Quality

Advertising and Quality Improvement

Professor Borden has dealt extensively with the question: Does advertising tend to improve the quality and range of merchandise? He makes two points:

First, advertising tends "decidedly" to improve the quality and range of merchandise.

Second, modern advertising has contributed to the high degree of product differentiation that exists at the present time. And such product differentiation which has at times been criticized as "meaningless often proves to be significant to some consumers."[1]

Quality of goods and services has been raised in North America because society became more affluent and it could afford better quality products and improved services. Advertising has spurred business firms on to the development of new products and improved products, "but profit on new products and improvements has generally been realized only as a result of aggressive cultivation of the market and of educating and influencing con-

---

[1] "The Economic Effects of Advertising", *op. cit.*, p. 277.

sumers to a realization of the satisfactions the new products would give."[2]

Professor Borden further explained: "In building consumer acceptance they (advertising and aggressive selling) have led to a relatively quick establishment of large-scale demand, upon which low prices have often depended. In turn, they have been a stimulant to product improvement."[3]

But advertising contributes not only to facilitating the acceptance by consumers of "good" products. It also helps in weeding out "bad" products. By speeding up this weeding-out process, advertising aids in the maximization of resources use and in minimizing wastefulness, a certain amount of which appears to be unavoidable in this age of rapid technological advancement and changes in consumer attitudes. The speed-up of the weeding-out process of "bad" products, and the benefits accruing to business in limiting losses, has been explained in these terms:

> Advertising is no cure-all for every sales slump. An excellent advertising campaign may not benefit an unsatisfactory product—indeed, the campaign may hasten the product's demise. This is because the investment in launching a new product is considerable. Months are spent on research, on market and product testing, on drawing up specifications for supplies, equipment and manufacture. To recoup this investment, the manufacturer usually depends not only on sales, but on repeat sales—and that means developing a host of satisfied customers. If the customers find that the product does not live up to their expectations, the strong probability is that they will refuse to buy again, and further, may become a powerful anti-sales force in the market. As a consequence, the product will perhaps soon disappear, and the manufacturer faced with a severe loss. The more people find out quickly that a product is inferior, the more rapidly we would expect sales to suffer. Thus, one effect of good advertising will often be to destroy a bad product.[4]

---

[2] *Ibid.*, p. 275.
[3] *Ibid.*
[4] *Proceedings* of the Special Joint Committee of the Senate and House of Commons on Consumer Credit (Prices), December 13, 1966, p. 1998.

Looking at Canadian developments over the last half of the century, as society became wealthier, the emphasis shifted from acquiring the necessities of life to obtaining a greater variety of goods and services with a new dimension added—much greater emphasis on quality and usefulness of newly developed products and services.

This growing interest in the performance and reliability of newly developed products led to the growing acceptance of brand-name items which gave the consumer the assurance that manufacturers and distributors of repute were standing behind the quality and serviceability of the product. As more and more brand-name products came on the market, a new problem developed: product differentiation.

Product Differentiation

Product differentiation refers to the modern marketing principle of providing consumers with a wide choice of competing articles to serve the same or similar purposes. One customary distinction is between brand-name products and private-brand products. "Brand-name products are produced and sold by manufacturers under an exclusive label. Private-brand products, also known as 'house' or 'stencil' brands, are promoted and sold by retailers under their own brand names and trade marks, and distribution is confined to outlets they control. The retailer may have his own production facilities for his private-brand product, or he may use a contract supplier who may also be a manufacturer of a national brand in the same category."[5]

It was as a result of development of brand-name products and the building up of confidence on the part of consumers in such products that advertising has been able to make a major contribution to the process of product differentiation.

Product differentiation in essence means providing consumers with an increased range of choices. The benefits of product

---

5 *Ibid.*, p. 2002.

differentiation for the consumer have been described in these terms:

(a) Greater variety of choice more likely to meet the specific preferences and needs of the consumer;
(b) Greater availability of products to meet consumer needs in terms of time and outlets;
(c) Improvements in product quality;
(d) Better services including warrantees and guarantees;
(e) Broader range of prices;
(f) Tendency to lower prices, or to restrain undue price rises.[6]

The critics of advertising say: If product differentiation is real, in the sense of differences in usefulness, quality, serviceability and price, then it performs a useful service by increasing consumer choice and making the system of competitive market mechanism more effective. To the extent that advertising makes a contribution to this process and provided that it does not lead to industrial concentration with possible adverse effects on consumer choice and prices, then advertising makes a positive contribution to the working of the economic system.

But in many instances, so the claim goes, product differentiation is only nominal. The differences in quality and serviceability are either non-existent, or so minute as to have little or no significance from the point of view of maximizing consumer satisfaction. If on top of this there is no significant price differential involved, or if there is an appearance of price differential given without this being in fact the case—as for example in a candy-bar wrapped in such a way as to give the appearance of a "larger" bar—then advertising serving such brand-name product differentiation may be misleading, socially undesirable and economically wasteful.

Brand-Name Products — Advantages

Responsible exponents of the merits of advertising, while not condoning misleading advertising, make the point that brand-

6 *Ibid.*

name product differentiation brings many advantages to the consumer which on balance not only offset some possible disadvantages, but in fact bring material net gains to the consumer and society as a whole. As Professor Borden explained:

> The desire of producers to offer under their specific brands products which will be preferred by consumers has led them to a constant experimentation with possible combinations of desirable product qualities. Technology has been called upon to develop new and improved products which some group of consumers might prefer. The quest is for the desirable product, but always management has in mind aggressively promoting the improved product and is influenced by its desires for ideas which it may use in its advertising and selling efforts. Thus, advertising and selling are an integral part of the system, and out of the system has come a tremendous range of merchandise.
>
> As part of the process of stimulating product differentiation, advertising has contributed to progress in merchandise improvements. As a result of the process of constantly offering new differentiations, enterprise has placed on the market improved products which better fill consumers' desires and needs than did previous products. This product improvement has been rapid and striking in the case of relatively new products, such as automobiles, radios, refrigerators, washing machines, and other mechanical contrivances. Over a relatively short period of years such products have been made far more efficient and dependable than those which preceded them and have been offered at prices which generally have been but a small fraction of the prices of earlier years. But even for merchandise long on the market, the improvement has been substantial over a period of time; this is true, for example, of products such as gasoline and sheeting, which at any one time appear to critics to be relatively standardized.[7]

As far as brand-name products are concerned, the latter do not assure the consumer of high quality in all instances. But, since successful business operations depend on "repeat" buying, businessmen have learned that assurance of quality and dependability is one means of keeping the consumer satisfied and

---

[7] "The Economic Effects of Advertising", *op. cit.*, p. 277.

retaining his loyalty to the brand-name product. Says Professor Borden:

> Although maintenance of brand quality is not entirely dependent upon advertising, nevertheless advertising has some influence because the advertised brand usually represents a goodwill asset which has been built at considerable expense, and injury to which would represent a business loss.[8]

The essence of the argument that advertising makes, on balance, a useful contribution to the maintenance and the improvement of quality, and that product differentiation is in the best interest of the consumer, is the acceptance of the principle of consumer choice in a wealthy economy like Canada's.

The reasoning is as follows: Canada is a wealthy country and incomes of consumers are rising. Consumers want a greater variety of goods and services to choose from. Who should say whether six varieties or twelve varieties of a particular product is the right number, or that there should be only one type of product in the interest of conserving resources, such as was practised during World War II?

Should the decision be made by a Government Department of Consumer Affairs, or perhaps the Department of Industry, telling business firms what to do and how many varieties of each product they may be permitted to produce? This would be tantamount to controlling production and distribution of such products, and it would significantly slow down new product and improved product development in the future.

Should a decision be made by industry agreeing among themselves? Such arrangements cannot help but be suspect of possible collusion, and the latter is unlikely to serve the best national interest.

Reliance on Market Forces

Or should the decision be left to the market-place, permitting the forces of competition to have their full play? For, if there is

---

8 *Ibid.*, pp. 276 and 277.

a point when product differentiation goes too far, then businessmen will soon find out that this effort does not pay. The result
will be that producers will concentrate more on the brands that
consumers prefer, and the rest of the brands will wither away.
And businessmen, if they do not want to lose money over the
long run, will sooner or later discard the production of such
items.

This is not to say that in the weeding-out process some social
waste does not occur. It does. It is a price that a wealthy society
like Canada's so far has been willing to pay. And there are no
indications that this attitude is likely to change. On the contrary,
the trend is in the direction of the Canadian income earner
becoming better off and demanding greater opportunities for
his right as a consumer to spend his money as he wants to.
Further, with rising educational levels, the consumer is likely
to become even more selective and insist on a greater range of
choice than has been open to him in the past.

There appears to be little public support in evidence in Canada
for turning over to Government control over product development and product differentiation, nor is there much support for
the suggestion that product differentiation should be limited as
a result of agreements reached by business firms themselves.

The professional advertisers make the claim that the benefits
of product differentiation in Canada far outweigh any possible
adverse effects and they call it—the alleged "waste" associated
with product differentiation—a "catalytic stimulant to economic
growth". To quote:

> Much product differentiation serves a constructive purpose
> by leading to product innovations and improvements. At any
> given point in time, some product differentiation may be only
> nominal. But over the longer term the cumulative effect of such
> distinctions may lead to significant improvements in quality of
> product and its value and satisfaction to the consumer. Further,
> the trend of innovations spurs on businessmen to continuously
> strive for product improvement and production economies
> through research and development.

Nominal product differentiation, some suggest, may involve social "waste". The alternative, however, would be to reduce product differentiation by artificial means which in the end may involve greater social costs than the system presently in operation in Canada. The alleged "waste" indeed may be regarded as part of the catalytic stimulant to economic growth in a largely private enterprise-oriented market-type economy like Canada's.[9]

Professor Borden concludes: "Only through trial and error in the market can progress be made in merchandise development."[10] Apparently a wealthy society whose people enjoy rising incomes and standards of living are willing to support the trial and error working of the market mechanism. Two reasons may be advanced:

1. Because a wealthy society can afford it.

2. Because whatever waste may be involved—and the extent of the waste has never been measured in aggregative terms, or proven for that matter in some other way affecting consumer spending as a whole—the alternative of a significant degree of Government control over the production and distribution system in Canada or potentially collusive agreements among industries, has appeared to be distinctly less appealing to the Canadian people than the system presently in existence.

---

9 *Proceedings* of the Special Joint Committee of the Senate and House of Commons on Consumer Credit (Prices), December 13, 1966, p. 2003.
10 "The Economic Effects of Advertising", *op. cit.*, p. 277.

9

Innovation

Does Advertising Create Human Wants?

Innovations involve the production of new goods or the creation of new services, the altering of existing goods and services so as to create new or added consumer satisfaction and a multitude of other economic activities which result in meeting new wants in new ways, or existing wants in improved ways.

What is the role of advertising in new want creation? Does it facilitate the introduction of innovations, which is one major way of contributing to new want creation?

One economist explained the complexity of want determination and the effect of advertising on it in these terms:

> Human wants are numerous, complex, imperfectly known, and frequently changing. . . . Advertisers are constantly trying to discover what people want, or to guess what they may want; to suggest new wants, or even to persuade people that they want things when they don't really want them at all. True or false, the want must be there, or be thought to be there.[1]

The implication is that advertising may influence human wants. But wants themselves are created by people who are

---

[1] *Advertising, A New Approach, op. cit.,* pp. 7 and 9.

affected by a multitude of factors including education, cultural background, social strata, community environment, economic capacity, etc.

Professional views differ on this subject. One of the outstanding proponents of the school of thought that advertising is want-creating and that a good deal of it is "bad" or socially wasteful, is Professor J. K. Galbraith, well known for his book *The Affluent Society*. To quote:

> The even more direct link between production and wants is provided by the institutions of modern advertising and salesmanship. These cannot be reconciled with the notion of independently determined desires, for their central function is to create desires—to bring into being wants that previously did not exist.[2]

Professor Galbraith then proceeds to submit his own interpretation of the motivational process and its implications for the working of the economic system by saying that it is production and the need to sell goods and services produced that create wants. He reasons:

> If the individual's wants are to be urgent they must be original with himself. They cannot be urgent if they must be contrived for him. And above all they must not be contrived by the process of production by which they are satisfied. For this means that the whole case for the urgency of production, based on the urgency of wants, falls to the ground. One cannot defend production as satisfying wants if that production creates the wants. . . .
>
> If production creates the wants it seeks to satisfy, or if the wants emerge *pari passu* with the production, then the urgency of the wants can no longer be used to defend the urgency of the production. Production only fills a void that it has itself created.[3]

Based on this reasoning, Professor Galbraith develops a concept he calls the "Dependence Effect". By this he means

[2] *The Affluent Society*, by J. K. Galbraith, Houghton Mifflin Company, Boston, 1958, p. 155.
[3] *Ibid.*, pp. 152 and 153.

the manner in which the creation of wants is dependent on the process which satisfies them. Professor Galbraith offers this conclusion:

> As a society becomes increasingly affluent, wants are increasingly created by the process by which they are satisfied. This may operate passively. Increases in consumption, the counterpart of increases in production, act by suggestion or emulation to create wants. Or producers may proceed actively to create wants through advertising and salesmanship. Wants thus come to depend on output. In technical terms it can no longer be assumed that welfare is greater at an all-round higher level of production than at a lower one. It may be the same. The higher level of production has, merely, a higher level of want creation necessitating a higher level of want satisfaction.[4]

The implication of Professor Galbraith's reasoning, presented in a simplified way, is: If production creates consumer wants, then a theory that the consumer is a primary determinant of his wants and thus "king" in the market-place is wanting. And the producer who performs both the function "of making the goods and of making the desires for them"[5] may be acting in his best interests and not in the best interests of the consumer.

If this is the case, advertising as part of the techniques used to persuade the consumer to buy, becomes suspect, and this explains "why advertising has so long been regarded with such uneasiness by economists".[6]

Another economist, while acceding the social usefulness of advertising if it performs the function of informing the consuming public, says that to the extent that it "seeks to persuade", advertising may be considered "a waste of resources". Professor Richard Caves observes:

> Advertising has its good and bad points. On the good side, it informs us of the goods available and tells us about market

---

[4] *Ibid.*, p. 158.
[5] *Ibid.*, p. 156.
[6] *Ibid.*, p. 157.

conditions so that we know where to go for the lowest price or the model best suited to our needs. To this extent, advertising makes markets more perfect than they otherwise would be. On the other hand, much advertising aims not to inform but to misinform us. It seeks to change our preference patterns and create wants which our private introspections would deny. It aims at making us believe statements which may be scientifically unverifiable or false. At the point where advertising departs from its function of informing and seeks to persuade or deceive us, it tends to become a waste of resources.[7]

The following quotation illustrates the opposite point of view held by professionals in the field:

> Advertising is accused of creating wants. This is not a true picture; advertising evokes and activates latent wants, which people never realized they had the means of satisfying. The failures of marketing almost always reside in the failure to assess rightly whether a true want exists. You cannot create a want which does not exist.[8]

In modern society wants are continuously changing and multiplying. They may be stimulated by new discoveries, new goods coming onto the market, new services offered to the consumer.

Producers use advertising to inform consumers about new possibilities of meeting old wants or satisfying new wants.

Wants and Innovations

The techniques and processes that contribute to creating new wants are innovations. Advertising attempts to put across the innovations to the consumer. It does not create innovations.

Advertising may pave the way for the acceptance of innovations. From the businessman's point of view, advertising will be judged successful if the consumer is prepared to accept the new product or the new service. But if he rejects it, no amount of advertising can, over the long run, force the consumer to

---

7 *American Industry: Structure, Conduct, Performance, op. cit.*, p. 102.
8 *The Influence and Techniques of Modern Advertising, op. cit.*, p. 5.

continue buying items against his better judgment, for the consumer has certain built-in safeguards which ensure that good judgment prevails in the end (see Chapter 11).

This is not to say that consumers, entrepreneurs and advertisers may not make mistakes, as well as the professional advertising advisers such as advertising agencies, which assist in the formulation of advertising campaigns. They all make mistakes, some more often than others. But in the final result the consumer remains the determining factor in a market-oriented type of economy such as Canada's. Recognition of this reality is essential to successful business operations in North America.

Theory of Innovation

The economist who first presented the theory of innovation was Joseph A. Schumpeter. He defined innovation as the "introduction of new commodities . . . technological change in the production of commodities already in use, the opening up of new markets or of new sources of supply, taylorization of work, improved handling of material, the setting up of new business organizations such as department stores—in short, any 'doing things differently' in the realm of economic life."[9]

Schumpeter explains that the process of innovation is one of the dynamic factors of economic growth in a largely private enterprise and market-oriented economy, and its many effects on economic and social progress fall into three main categories:

1. Innovations contribute significantly to expanding investment in plant and equipment, essential to raising the productive capacity of the country, and to providing rising levels of employment and income by making use of increased savings.[10]

2. Innovations contribute to increasing the number of business firms, as new vigorous firms take the place of older

---

[9] *Business Cycles*, by Joseph A. Schumpeter, McGraw-Hill Book Company, Inc., New York, 1939, Volume 1, p. 84.
[10] *Ibid.*, p. 93.

firms which are going out of business because of "their inability to keep up the pace in innovating which they themselves had been instrumental in setting in the time of their vigor."[11]

3. Innovations contribute to bringing to the fore "New Men", the business leaders who have the vision, enterprise and determination to try new ideas and to implant their stamp on economic and social progress of society.[12]

Businessmen introduce innovations if they can expect that these will turn out to be profitable over the longer term. Such decisions to proceed are made, according to Schumpeter, within a framework he calls "horizon", that is "a range of choice" based on expectations "of profitability and foresight".[13]

If entrepreneurs consider introducing innovations they may turn to advertising to facilitate the acceptance of these innovations. This is one way in which businessmen endeavour to reduce the risks involved in incurring capital and developmental expenditures and improving their chances for a profitable venture.

Many economists have accepted Schumpeter's innovation theory and its implications for advertising. To quote one American economist who follows both Professor Schumpeter's and Professor Borden's reasoning:

> Advertising, by acquainting the consumer with the values of new products, widens the market for these products, pushes forward their acceptance by the consumer, and encourages the investment and entrepreneurship necessary for innovation.[14]

While the view that advertising facilitates the public acceptance of innovations and thus makes a constructive contribution to continuing economic growth has been increasingly accepted by economists—though at the same time the criticism of some of the adverse effects of advertising has also grown—the fact

---

11 *Ibid.*, p. 95.
12 *Ibid.*, p. 96.
13 *Ibid.*, p. 99.
14 *Some Comments on the Role of Advertising in the American Economy—A Plea for Revaluation, op cit.*, p. 10.

remains that very little empirical research has been undertaken to verify this thesis. This point has been emphasized in these terms:

> Advertising . . . holds out the promise of a greater and speedier return than would occur without such methods, thus stimulating investment, growth, and diversity. But no one apparently has been able to measure quantitatively the benefits of this function, to weigh against those deficiencies for which attempts have been made to make measurements.[15]

Product Originator

Following Schumpeter, innovations may take many forms. One of these, the creation of new products is singled out here for examination. The question is: How does advertising affect the acceptance of the new product by the consumer?

When an entrepreneur brings a new product onto the market he incurs certain development and capital expenditures. He charges a price for the product which enables him to recover the cost of production plus any losses he may have incurred in the earlier period of introduction plus a profit and a net return on his investment or that of his shareholders.[16]

The entrepreneur who brings a new product to the market or creates a new service is a product originator who has taken the initiative and the risks involved. He will endeavour to obtain acceptance of the new product by whatever promotional means he believes will serve this purpose, and this as a rule may include a carefully planned advertising program. To achieve consumer acceptance, he will aim at product differentiation by building up a brand-name item. He will endeavour to create in the minds of the consumers a confidence factor in the quality, usefulness and serviceability of the product, and he will attempt

---

[15] *Ibid.*

[16] In most Canadian companies, management which sets price policies —and this applies mainly to large corporations—is separate from investors, who provide the capital funds but who as a rule have little influence on operating policies.

to achieve continuity in consumers' acceptance of this product. He will endeavour to achieve all this while charging a price for the product which will enable him to recoup his costs and, in addition, to make a profit and return on investment, as mentioned above.

For a while, the product originator may have the market to himself. But as the market expands, other firms will enter it. These may be firms which have come forward with a similar product with a different brand-name. These brand-name product competitors will try to obtain their share of the expanding market by heavy advertising and other means.

Sooner or later, however, a new type of competitor will enter the market. He is the product imitator. Who is he? What does he do? Does he perform a useful social function?

Product Imitator

The product imitator brings to the market either the identical product or a product very similar to a brand-name product, though it may not be identical in quality and performance to the brand-name product.

The product imitator may spend little or no money on research and product development. He may incur modest or no advertising expenditures in launching his products. He may give the impression that his product is as good as the one marketed under a brand-name. He may not give the same warranty or service as the brand-name product distributor.

The production and distribution costs of the product imitator would of necessity be lower than those of the product originator. Hence he will be able to sell his non-brand-name product at a lower price. The reason he can do so has been explained by Professor Borden in these terms:

> Their (imitators') entry into the market and the elasticity
> of demand which they exploit are made possible by the

aggressive selling efforts of innovators. In short, the imitators often ride on the coat-tails of the innovators.[17]

Lower prices are the product imitators' strongest means of appealing to the consumer. They may take away some of the business of the product originator as well as that of other brand-name distributors. But product imitators may also reach consumers in lower income brackets who may have been precluded from buying the higher priced brand-name products.

Effect of Advertising
on New Product Acceptance

To return now to the question: How does advertising affect the acceptance of new products or services by the consumer?

The answer given is: Advertising informs the consumer of the new product availability and it presents as persuasive a case as advertisers know how to consumers to purchase the new items brought to the market. In so doing, advertising aims at increasing the acceptance of the commodity by the consumer. Even after the product originator has achieved consumer acceptance of his new product, he will continue to advertise heavily—though there may be variations in advertising budgets from time to time—to keep product differentiation continuously before the consumer and to ensure his share of the consumer dollar. At a later stage, as and when the product imitator enters the market, considerably less advertising, if any at all, is required to sell the products of the product imitator.

Thus advertising assists both the product originator and the product imitator. It helps the former in achieving consumer acceptance of his product. It helps the latter in benefiting from the consumer acceptance that has been built up in advertising the brand-name product.

Most of the advertising costs will in the first instance have been borne by the product originator. In the end the cost of

---

17 "The Economic Effects of Advertising", *op. cit.*, p. 266.

advertising will be incorporated in the final price charged to the consumer, whose main benefits are a wider range of choice of products, increasing competition, and lower prices that may result therefrom, a point developed further in Chapter 13.

Social Function of Product Imitator

The constructive contribution of the product originator is referred to in several sections of this study (see particularly Chapter 10). It may be useful to consider in this context the question whether the product imitator performs a socially useful function.

Brand-name product manufacturers and distributors are frequently critical of the business practices of product imitators. They mention inferior quality of product, lack of warranty, inadequate or no service, deceptive advertising, etc. But looking at the activities of product imitators from a social point of view, they should be given credit for being more than "coat-tail" riders. Product imitators perform certain socially useful services and these include:

1. "By keeping his selling and marketing costs low and by offering consumers the option of low prices, (the product imitator) serves to help hold down competition in advertising and other non-price forms. In short, he serves to help bring low costs and low prices in established industries."[18]

2. By offering lower priced products, the product imitator extends the range of potential consumers.

3. By successfully appealing to consumers, the product imitator provides increased competition to the product originator, spurring on the latter to further innovations (see Chapter 13).

---

[18] *Ibid.*, p. 267.

10

Investment

Advertising and Mass Markets

The point has been made in Chapter 9 that advertising facilitates the introduction of innovations, among other things, by encouraging consumer acceptance of new products and services that may come on the market.

Innovations, in turn, are introduced into economic life usually through undertaking capital projects involving expenditures for plant and equipment, etc. Capital expenditures are not made only to introduce new products or market improved products, however. Large capital expenditures are also made to increase the productivity of manufacturing operations and the distributive system (as well as in other sectors) so as to enable business firms to remain competitive, not only in competition against like products but also against alternative products and services that compete for the consumer dollar.

The prime aim of most business firms in their efforts of profit maximization is to obtain access to as large a market as money, ingenuity and foresight, as well as a good product or service permit. As and when a mass market for a given product can be achieved, the advantages of large-scale production and distribution will enable the entrepreneur to reap some of its benefits, which may take the form of lower costs and higher profits. In many cases, the businessman may share the benefits from higher productivity with other factors of production, particularly labour and capital, and with the consumer, in terms of lower prices or the avoidance or lessening of price increases which may otherwise have become necessary.

Advertising and Risk Minimization

Advertising is one means businessmen use to achieve mass markets, to maximize profits and to minimize risks. And mass markets are needed if mass production is to take place. And mass production is needed to achieve some of the economies it may yield and the additional jobs it may provide.

Production economies, to the extent they are passed on to the consumer, may mean lower prices to him and/or higher real income to the income earner. Additional job opportunities are essential if employment is to be found for the increases in the labour force and workers replaced by technological change.

The contribution which advertising makes to encourage investment and to assist businessmen in minimizing their risk-taking activities has been explained by Professor Borden in these terms:

> While changes in social conditions and the forces of selling provide an explanation of growth of wants and willingness of the population to consume, this willingness could not have been satisfied had not the productive machine been called into existence. The productive machine which makes the products available provides the consumer income with which to purchase products. The existence of both the products and the income of consumers depends upon risk-taking by businessmen who see an opportunity for profit through making and selling goods which they think consumers will want. Their risk-taking activities bring the investment in factory and production facilities, which not only produce goods for consumption but employ labor and pay the wages and the return on capital upon which con-

sumer income depends. In short, the activities of entrepreneurs create the markets for their own products.

Advertising and aggressive selling have an influence upon investment because they are important integral parts of the system which leads to investment. Advertising and aggressive selling in themselves have not been the causes of the launching of new enterprises, or of the expansion of old, but they have been important elements whereby the new or enlarged enterprises might hope to gain a profitable demand. They frequently have been helpful in speeding up a demand which has called for increasing investment. They have promised the stability of demand and of profit to an enterprise which is attractive to investment. By such means have factories been built, men employed, and the products and incomes for increasing consumer satisfactions been established.

While advertising and aggressive selling have probably had greatest influence upon investment in new industries, they have also played a part in helping to increase the demand of established industries, which has called for investment to expand productive facilities. Even in the case of declining industries, the selling force has been employed to try to hold demand and thus to protect the investment in those industries against the inroads of the new industries. In some instances selling has also served to stimulate demand for new improvements in the products of declining industries and thus has served to give to the industry a new life cycle calling for investment.[1]

Advertising as Insurance

To re-state two ways in which advertising will affect investment:[2]

1. By expanding markets or at least safe-guarding existing markets for established products, businessmen will be assured of the worthwhileness of new capital investment they may be considering.

---

[1] "The Economic Effects of Advertising", *op. cit.*, pp. 278 and 279.
[2] Again the reference here is only to consumer advertising and the investment that may follow in consequence of such spending.

2. By assisting in the realization of markets for new or improved products, the risks that businessmen face in proceeding with a new venture may be minimized.

In this sense, advertising is sometimes looked at as an insurance against failure. But whether businessmen look at advertising as a sales aid to reach a market large enough for profitable operations or as an insurance to minimize risks, the end result may be the same: businessmen may proceed with a new venture and make the necessary capital expenditures. Hence, whatever the motivation on the part of the entrepreneurs, there appears to be a link between advertising and investment.

Interaction of Advertising and Investment

This interaction between advertising and investment has far-reaching implications for economic and social progress, particularly in North America where both advertising and investment have reached higher levels than on any other continent in the world.

The benefits from rising capital investment are now widely accepted—its contribution to increasing employment and income and to insuring continuing economic growth and improvement in the standard of living as well as the means of introducing new technological developments so essential to keep the economy dynamic. But the contribution that advertising makes to facilitating an increasing volume of business investment is less clear-cut and less widely accepted. Some critics claim that some of the benefits of advertising thus obtained are more than offset by disadvantages (see Chapter 3).

Professor Borden, after careful investigation, came out on the side of those who believe that the positive contribution which advertising makes to encourage investment outweighs some of its disadvantages. To quote:

> Advertising and aggressive selling as integral parts of the free competitive system have been a significant force in increasing the investment in productive facilities and in advancing

the technology of production, two developments which have largely accounted for the fourfold increase of real national income per capita during the past 100 years.[3]

Advertising Expenditures and Capital Investment

How close is the link between investment and advertising? Again, little quantitative evidence exists to answer this question. To deal with this question, more than quantitative evidence is needed, for analysis has to probe into causal relationship and into business motivation. How do businessmen decide what advertising budgets are required to establish a market of a given size which will warrant the undertaking of additional capital investment? How do businessmen decide what type of advertising campaign and what kind of advertising media will likely come closest to minimizing their risks and enhancing their prospects for a successful venture which in turn would justify for them proceeding with the investment?

In the field of statistical information, data are also lacking to assess trends of comparable flows such as advertising expenditures on consumer goods and services. Information is needed not only in terms of total expenditures but also for comparable flows, that is by industries, sectors, large corporations and the main commodity groupings.

Available data permit nothing but the broadest kind of generalization, and even these must be qualified because the flows that are measured cover different sectors of economic activity. Still, some trends can be observed and these have a certain meaning because the data are comparable over time as they relate to each sector.

The comparison presented here covers trends of total advertising expenditures, i.e. business, institutional and government advertising, and trends of business gross capital formation, as

---

[3] *Ibid.* p. 277.

per National Accounts. The latter cover for Canada capital expenditures by private and government business enterprises (on plant and equipment), private non-commercial institutions, and outlay on new residential construction by individuals and business investors. The U.S. data relate to Gross Private Domestic Investment, which covers a similar sector as does Business Gross Capital Formation in Canada. The pertinent data are presented for both Canada and the United States for the period 1946 to 1966 in Table 2.

In Canada, Business Gross Capital Formation reached a level of $12.2 billion in 1966, about 8 times the level of twenty years before. Advertising expenditures reached a level 6 times that of 1946.

In the United States the situation is quite different. Both capital expenditures and advertising expenditures rose at similar rates over the period 1946-1966, to close to 5 times the level in the recent period as compared with the immediate postwar period.

Two questions arise:

1. Why did advertising expenditures rise less rapidly than capital investment in Canada?

2. Why did both advertising expenditures and capital investment in Canada rise more rapidly than the corresponding expenditures in the United States?

The answer to the first question, in the absence of further research, is of necessity quite tentative. One possible explanation would be that costs of construction, machinery and equipment, which make up capital spending, rose more rapidly than did costs of advertising.[4]

---

[4] Again no satisfactory price indices are available to measure changes in the cost of advertising. The advertising industry claims that its prices have risen less rapidly than have prices of capital goods, but such claims await adequate statistical verification in Canada. In the United States, *Media/Scope* publishes monthly advertising cost indexes for five communication media.

Table 2

BUSINESS GROSS CAPITAL FORMATION AND ADVERTISING
EXPENDITURES, CANADA AND UNITED STATES, 1946-1966

| Year | CANADA | | | UNITED STATES | | |
| | BUSINESS GROSS CAPITAL FORMATION[1] ($ millions) | ADVERTISING EXPENDITURES[2] | | GROSS PRIVATE DOMESTIC INVESTMENT ($ millions) | ADVERTISING EXPENDITURES | |
		Total ($ millions)	Percentage of Business Gross Capital Formation		Total ($ millions)	Percentage of Gross Private Domestic Investment[3]
1946	1,388	130.9	9.4	24.2	3,364	13.9
1947	2,085	158.4	7.6	34.4	4,260	12.4
1948	2,619	183.1	7.0	41.3	4,864	11.8
1949	3,032	211.1	7.0	38.8	5,202	13.4
1950	3,348	234.0	7.0	47.3	5,710	12.1
1951	3,959	262.3	6.6	49.0	6,426	13.1
1952	4,451	292.3	6.6	48.8	7,156	14.7
1953	4,998	331.4	6.6	52.1	7,809	15.0
1954	4,779	363.4	7.6	53.3	8,164	15.3
1955	5,210	401.0	7.7	61.4	9,194	15.0
1956	6,774	463.3	6.8	65.3	9,905	15.2
1957	7,335	490.6	6.7	66.5	10,311	15.5
1958	6,975	517.0	7.4	62.4	10,302	16.5
1959	6.894	555.8	8.1	70.5	11,117	15.8
1960	6,692	584.1	8.7	71.3	11,932	16.7
1961	6,635	600.8	9.1	69.7	11,845	17.0
1962	6,960	631.6	9.1	77.0	12,381	16.1
1963	7,591	659.9	8.7	81.3	13,107	16.1
1964	9,103	700.7	7.7	88.3	14,155	16.0
1965	10,424	760.6	7.3	97.5	15,120	15.5
1966[4]	12,200	821.0	6.7	116.5	16,500	14.2
Percentage Increases						
1946-1951	185.2	100.4	—	102.5	91.0	—
1951-1956	71.1	76.6	—	33.3	54.1	—
1956-1961	−2.2	29.7	—	6.7	19.6	—
1961-1966	83.9	36.7	—	67.1	39.3	—
1946-1966	779.0	527.2	—	381.4	390.4	—

[1] Includes capital expenditures by private and government business enterprises, private non-commercial institutions and outlays on new residential construction by individuals and business investors.

[2] Includes advertising commissions.

[3] Covers capital expenditures in fixed assets, including outlays on private structures (including engineering works), producers' durable equipment and residential structures. The concept covers approxi-

(Footnote continued on next page)

Another explanation is that many capital expenditures are made independent of the provision for advertising budgets. Furthermore, many products such as raw materials or basic agricultural products (e.g. wheat), or industrial machinery and equipment can be sold without any, or with comparatively little, advertising. Hence, whenever the structure of capital spending moves in the direction of greater emphasis on resources development, basic food production and capital goods industries, increases in advertising may fall short of increases in capital investment.

But even in industries where advertising expenditures are substantial in relation to capital investment, there is no *a priori* justification for pre-supposing that advertising expenditures must of necessity rise in some predetermined and predeterminable relationship to capital investment. Advertising budgets are formulated in relation to market penetration desired by the entrepreneur and not in relation to the capital investment required to serve the market.

If some of the reasons advanced explain the differentials in the rates of growth as between advertising expenditures and

mately the same type of expenditures as listed in the Canadian National Accounts as "Business Gross Fixed Capital Formation".

4 Preliminary estimates.

Source: CANADA—data of Business Gross Fixed Capital Formation for 1946-1965 from *National Accounts, Income and Expenditure, 1965,* and earlier issues; data of advertising expenditures from the *Report* of the Royal Commission on Publications, Queen's Printer, Ottawa, 1961, from *Printing and Publishing Industry,* 1964, and *Radio and Television Broadcasting,* 1964, Dominion Bureau of Statistics, Ottawa, 1966, and earlier issues; and supplementary estimates from MacLean-Hunter Research Bureau, *A Report on Advertising Revenues in Canada,* Toronto, October 1966; "Gross Ad Revenues Expected to Go Up", *Marketing,* November 25, 1966, p. 79. UNITED STATES—data of Gross Private Domestic Investment for 1946-1965 from *Economic Report of the President, January 1966,* and *Economic Indicators, December 1966,* prepared for the Joint Economic Committee by the Council of Economic Advisers, United States Government Printing Office, Washington, D.C., 1966; data on advertising expenditures 1946 to 1965 from *Statistical Abstracts of the United States,* U.S. Department of Commerce, United States Government Printing Office, Washington, D.C., 1966; the 1966 estimate is from "The Strategy: Market for Growth", *Printers Ink,* January 13, 1967, p. 9; all other data are special estimates.

capital investment in Canada, the question arises as to why this observation is not borne out by the trends indicated for the United States; for in this country, spending on advertising and business investment has over the post-World War II period as a whole risen at about similar rates, though there have been significant differences over the several quinquennial periods which make up the last two decades (see Table 2).

Again only tentative answers are possible at this stage. As has been explained in Chapter 5, American industry is more accustomed than Canadian industry to relying on advertising as the most economic means of reaching existing markets or developing new markets. American consumers in turn may be more prone to accept advertising as the most practical way of learning more about alternative choices open to individuals and families to satisfy their wants.

With both business and the consumer relying more on advertising, a somewhat closer relationship may be assumed to exist between advertising and investment than would be the case in a country where business is somewhat more cautious and the consumer somewhat more conservative. To some extent, this differentiation reflects variations in business and consumer attitudes in the United States and Canada.

There is another noteworthy feature indicated in the data shown in Table 2. During the last five years, Canada has continued to increase capital investment at a more rapid rate than the United States, partly because of a more rapid growth of the Canadian market as compared with the U.S. market and partly because of the greater capital intensity which characterizes many of Canada's major industries, particularly in the fields of national resources development, power and transportation.[5]

---

5 Other factors contributing to the relatively heavy use of capital equipment per employed person in Canada, as compared with the United States, includes higher capital overhead because of shorter production runs in Canada, less intensive use of facilities available, greater seasonal swings because of different weather conditions, more sparsely settled areas requiring greater capital investment in trans-

(Footnote continued on next page)

Business capital expenditures in Canada rose by 84 per cent over the period 1961-1966, as compared with 67 per cent for the United States. At the same time, advertising expenditures in Canada rose more slowly—37 per cent as compared with 39 per cent in the United States. This is contrary to the trend of the earlier postwar period when Canada was trying slowly but more or less continually to narrow somewhat the wide gap of per capita spending in advertising that exists between the two countries (see Chapter 4).

Again more research is needed to establish the reasons, (a) for the change in rates of advertising growth between the two countries, and (b) for the effect that this change has had and may have in the future on the general economic growth of the two countries as well as on the rate of expansion of business investment.

A comparison of the ratios of advertising expenditures to capital investment over the last twenty years suggests that this proportion varied for Canada between 7 and 9 per cent. The corresponding ratio for the United States moved in the 12 to 17 per cent range. Here is some more tentative indication of the somewhat lesser role that advertising plays in Canada in affecting the course, pattern and extent of investment than appears to be the case in the United States.

If subsequent research should confirm this tentative conclusion, then an implication would be that investment, which is a major income-creating factor, is less dependent on advertising expenditures in Canada than is the case in the United States. And if it is a rapid increase in money income, unaccompanied by corresponding increases in productivity, that may be a major factor adding to inflationary pressures—of the cost-push variety —then advertising appears to play a lesser role in Canada than in the United States in contributing to this situation.

portation and communication facilities, etc. (See *Second Annual Review, op. cit.*, pp. 59 and 60.)

11

Consumer

Principle of Division of Labour

Advertising involves an impersonal effort on the part of business to persuade consumers to buy certain commodities or services. It is distinct from personal selling in that the latter relies heavily on the personality of the salesman and the subjective impact he may have on a potential buyer. Against this, advertising relies mainly on the general appeal of the commercial message addressed to all consumers with equal effect, though the impact of the message may vary depending on the economic circumstances and the preferences of the consumer, and whether the advertisement is addressed to a general audience or to a specialized group. The impact of the advertising message will vary between media, depending on the objective. If demonstration is required then television will have the greatest impact. Further, television comes closer to personal selling than any other medium.

The initiative to advertise rests as a rule with the business-man who spends money on advertising to build up a market, and to gain or retain consumer acceptance of his product.

The consumer plays a passive role in the advertising process. His position is one of response or lack of response to the advertising message. If the response is negative, businessmen will either alter the advertising message, turn to other promotional and selling devices, or change the product or its price in an effort to obtain a positive response from consumers.

The reason why in a market- and largely private enterprise-oriented economy, like Canada's, the function of advertising has become the responsibility of the seller is based on a fundamental economic principle: division of labour.

It is more economic from society's point of view for the seller to tell the buyer what choices he has to spend his money, than for the buyer to seek out the seller to learn what consumer goods are for sale and at what price. That used to be the case, and still is the case, when a buyer visits a produce market, a trade fair, or other types of exhibitions. But speaking in general terms, the principle of division of labour in modern society has largely assigned the task of initiating advertising to the seller, simply because it is more economic to do so, and further because the seller, by serving his own self-interest, also serves the interest of the consumer.

As Professor Johnson explained:

> The seller has the resources and the economic incentive to provide the information; the buyer has not. The buyer has the further advantage that he need not pay for the information (by buying the product) unless he wants to. He is exposed, however, to the danger that the seller will deceive him; but he has the defenses that he need not buy the product again if he does not find it satisfactory, that he need not buy it the first time if he knows anyone who has done so and is dissatisfied, and that he can form a judgment on the truth and reliability of the seller's appeal to him by listening to the messages of rival sellers.[1]

The principle of division of labour has led to further specialization. Business firms employ experts in the fields of marketing, research and advertising, all providing specialized services designed to assist management to achieve the objective of selling

---

[1] *The Canadian Quandary, op. cit.,* p. 289.

more goods and services and doing so in the most economic manner possible.

One group of such specialists are advertising agencies which provide professional services to business firms and to other sectors of society to assist users of advertising to obtain the maximum benefits from such promotional efforts. Thus advertising agencies are concerned with ensuring "that advertising expenditures obtain maximum effectiveness". To achieve this objective, advertising agencies "are continuously endeavouring to improve the services" they render to their clients "and to follow certain principles of professional and ethical conduct".[2]

Advertising agencies are specialists "in the arts of persuasion". They consider it to be their "responsibility to be knowledgeable in the ways in which persuasion can influence people".[3]

The advertising profession claims that "technological achievement . . . married to persuasion" has been an important factor in Canada in contributing to "broaden the standard of living and to raise it to such a high level . . . the second highest in the world."[4]

The point then advanced by the advertising profession is that "persuasion", far from being a negative influence in diminishing social welfare, is a major positive factor contributing to enhancing the consumer's well-being through improving his standard of living, not only quantitatively, but also qualitatively by creating "comfort" and "convenience".[5]

---

[2] Proceedings of the Special Joint Committee of the Senate and House of Commons on Consumer Credit (Prices), December 13, 1966, *op. cit.*, p. 1995.

[3] Statement by C. Warren Reynolds, Director, Institute of Canadian Advertising, *Proceedings* of the Special Joint Committee of the Senate and House of Commons on Consumer Credit (Prices), December 13, 1966, p. 2054.

[4] *Ibid.*

[5] *Ibid.*

The difference of views held by members of the advertising profession as against views held by a number of members of the economist profession should be noted. The former say that the "persuasive" effect of advertising is essential to economic progress and to the enhancement of the consumer's welfare; the latter say that it may contribute to economic waste and misallocation of resources (see Chapter 1).

Who is right?

Advertising and the Consumer Interest

Businessmen advertise primarily for reasons of self-interest. Thus they cannot be considered to be objective in formulating the advertising message and in choosing the means of communicating it to consumers. Given then that it is largely the profit motive that guides businessmen to advertise, the question arises: Does advertising also serve the consumer interest?

Generally the answer has been in the affirmative, though numerous objections have been raised against this premise on the ground that there are many circumstances where advertising may act to the detriment of consumers. In fact, most of the 33 criticisms listed in Chapter 3 belong in the category of claims of advertising not serving the best interests of consumers.

The essence of the criticism is that businessmen are prone to take advantage of the consumer. And, if the consumers' interests are a primary objective of economic policy—and most economists would be inclined to support this—then the question arises: Is the consumer in North America really as defenceless as some of the critics of advertising make out to be the case?

An answer to this question revolves around four points:

1. Self-defence mechanism of the consumer.
2. Competition.
3. Public control and regulation.
4. Consumer education.

Self-Defence Mechanism of Consumer

Professor Taplin has listed a number of factors as forming part of the self-defence mechanism that enables the consumer to resist some of the persuasive appeals addressed to him by advertisers.

1. The consumer's spending power is limited as of a point of time and over a period of time. Advertising may affect the consumer's choice of individual commodities, but it is not likely to succeed in persuading the consumer to spend more in aggregate than he is prepared to do.

2. The sheer weight and multiplicity of advertising appeals is such that the consumer "cannot respond to all of them and probably develops a resistance to the whole mass."[6]

3. Consumers develop habits of thought of what they consider "a reasonable price". While a period of strong inflationary pressures may affect such habits, they "remain a formidable obstacle to any seller who thinks he can succeed by advertising alone."[7]

4. Consumers develop certain associations with brand-name products and quality, and they may not repeat purchases if disappointed in the performance of the product.

5. Consumers have a "will to save" and the latter "implies some resistance by the saver to the persuasions of those who want him to spend."[8]

6. Consumers have a built-in aversion to "extravagant or misleading advertisements", with the result that businessmen using such advertisements will in the end defeat the very purpose of using advertising as a means of sales promotion.[9]

---

6 *Advertising, A New Approach, op. cit.*, p. 126.
7 *Ibid.*, p. 127.
8 *Ibid.*
9 The reasons listed under points 6. and 7. are advanced by John Hobson (see "The Social and Economic Context of Advertising", *op. cit.*, p. 7).

7. Most consumers who see or hear advertisements "are well aware that they are being sold something, and they discount a large measure of what is said."[10]

8. Consumers, as a rule, will take with a grain of salt such claims that a particular brand presents the "best" product, and thus will develop a loyalty to only that brand-name product which in their judgment "is indeed best for them".[11]

Competition

Businessmen are vying for the consumer dollar. They want to persuade the consumer to buy their products. Hence, the consumer's greatest ally in getting the best possible service and the lowest price is the businessman who wants to obtain his patronage. And the process through which most businessmen endeavour to obtain what they consider a reasonable share of the consumer dollar is through competition. This subject is discussed more fully in Chapter 15.

Public Control and Regulation

Public control and regulation of advertising offers the consumer protection in several ways:

1. Through the administration of the Federal Combines Investigation Act.[12] The purpose of this legislation is to assist in maintaining free and open competition as a prime stimulus to the achievement of maximum production, distribution and employment in a system of free enterprise. To this end, the legislation seeks to eliminate certain practices in restraint of trade that serve to prevent the nation's economic resources from being most effectively used for the advantage of all citizens.

---

10 *Ibid.*
11 The reason listed under item 8 above is advanced by Wroe Alderson (see *Dynamic Marketing Behaviour, op. cit.,* p. 123).
12 The Combines Investigation Act was first enacted in 1923 and subsequently amended in 1935, 1937, 1946, 1949, 1951, 1952, and finally consolidated in 1960.

The substantive provisions of the legislation are contained in Sections 2, 32, 33, 33A, 33B, 33C and 34 of the Combines Investigation Act. Two of the sections make specific references to advertising: Section 33B mentions suppliers granting advertising allowances; and Section 34, dealing with loss leaders, mentions "bait advertising" and "misleading advertising".

2.   Through the administration of a number of federal statutes which vest power into the Government and its regulatory or administrative agencies to deal with misleading advertising or other types of advertising that are not considered to be in the public interest. Such legislation covers specific commodities, as for example the regulations administered under the Food and Drug Act, the Opium and Narcotics Control Act and the Proprietary and Patent Medicine Act.

Other legislation relates to specific communication media, as for example, radio and television. Advertising on these media is subject to regulation and examination by the Board of Broadcast Governors. For example, under Section 11 of the Broadcasting Act of 1958, the Board administers regulations concerning the character of advertising and the amount of time to be devoted to advertising.

3.   Through the administration of provincial statutes concerning the advertising of certain items, such as the sale of alcoholic beverages.

Potentially, administration of the Combines Investigation Act may have the largest impact on the role of advertising in the Canadian economy and on the maintenance of the competitive system which provides the consumer with the greatest protection against advertising excesses or restraints of trade.

The above listing of the control and regulation of advertising by public authorities would not be complete if reference were not made also to the control of advertising standards, developed by industry itself, the communication media and the advertising agencies. Critics of advertising do not fully accept the efficacy of private standard setting, but the fact remains that advertising standards in Canada, as in the United States and the United Kingdom, have been greatly improved and increasingly observed by major advertisers and communication media.

In this connection, it may be of interest to consider the provisions of the British Code of Advertising Practice which has been found to be a more effective means of advertising control than legislative or regulatory control.

Recently the sections of industry and commerce concerned with advertising have consolidated into a single code, *The British Code of Advertising Practice*, the various existing rules governing advertising claims, and have adopted—with the agreement of the principal media—the sanction that advertisements which offend these standards should be debarred from publication. The governing body is called the Advertising Standards Authority, formed half from advertising and half from non-advertising interests, with an independent Chairman. The executive body is called the Code of Advertising Practice Committee, which sets up the codes and deals with the cases arising under them. Then there is the Advertisement Investigation Department of the Advertising Association which investigates the validity of claims, and there are experts available on most subjects to advise on the facts. It is a system which, it is claimed, is as "water-tight" as it can be.[13]

Consumer Advertising Expenditures

There are no comprehensive statistics available in Canada of advertising expenditures aimed at informing and persuading consumers to buy goods and services. Partial data can be used to illustrate trends but their inadequacies must be borne in mind. This is another area urgently requiring collection of comprehensive and comparable statistics—the amounts Canadians spend on the various types of consumer advertising—and the interpreta-

---

13 Based on a lecture by John Hobson (see "The Social and Economic Context of Advertising", *op. cit.*, p. 7).

tion of these data in terms of the effects of consumer advertising expenditures on total personal spending of this kind. This would require, among other things, a commodity breakdown of advertising expenditures comparable to the breakdown of personal expenditures on consumer goods and services, available in the National Accounts.

A few of the limitations of data presently available should be noted. The figures shown below are a special compilation based on data of national advertising expenditures for specific commodities, as compiled by Elliot-Haynes Limited and published in *Marketing*.

Some of the commodity groups listed cover both consumer goods and industrial goods. The allocation of advertising expenditures to one or the other category includes an arbitrary element, the extent of which is not known. A number of categories of advertising expenditures were allotted to consumer advertising even though they appeared to include a significant component of industrial advertising. An example would be automobile advertising, which includes advertising of passenger cars and of trucks and buses. The latter two types should be included under industrial advertising but this was not possible because of the aggregative nature of the data available. Hence, the figures presented below are likely to overstate consumer advertising in absolute terms. The only justification for using them is to illustrate trends, rather than to consider the data as an adequate measurement of the different types of advertising activity.

The data are further limited in terms of coverage. Advertising expenditures not included in the compilation are: local, retail and classified advertising, and advertising by chains and department stores, radio and television stations, theatres or political parties.

The data cover four types of media: newspapers, periodicals, radio and television. They therefore exclude such other printed media as catalogues and direct mail advertising, and outdoor advertising, as well as a miscellany of other types of advertising.

Total advertising covered in this more limited survey amounts to $235 million, equivalent to a little over one-third of total gross advertising expenditures in Canada, which are estimated at $761 million for 1965 (see Table 1).

Bearing in mind the qualifications as set out above, the compilation suggests that over the period 1961-1965, advertising addressed to the consumer rose somewhat more rapidly than "other" advertising, mainly of the industrial kind (see below).

	1961 ($ millions)	1965 ($ millions)	Percentage Increase 1961-1965
Advertising on Consumer Goods and Services	147	212	44
Other Advertising	18	23	29
Total	165	235	42

Consumer Education

Consumer education involves providing the consumer with objective and disinterested information about the quality, serviceability and prices of goods and services, so as (1) to enable him to verify the claims made in business advertisements, and (2) to provide him with supplementary information which may assist in making rational choices of alternatives open to him. Consumer education may take place in schools, colleges or through voluntary associations.

Professor Borden emphasizes the desirability of developing stronger groups which would aim at spreading consumer education more widely than is presently the case. To quote:

> From the standpoint of maximizing consumer satisfactions, such movements and activities are deemed natural and desirable developments. As yet consumer education has made little headway, but it is gaining in strength.[14]

Mr. Turner, following Professor Johnson, makes a strong case for creating new sources of neutral consumer information. Speaking with the authority of the Assistant Attorney General of the

---

[14] "The Economic Effects of Advertising", op. cit., p. 286.

Anti-Trust Division of the U.S. Department of Justice, Mr. Turner recently made the point:

> I believe the most promising approach is to introduce new sources of consumer information. It is the extent of uncertainty about the relative merits of competing products which contributes to the large effect of advertising, and this suggests that Government policies be directed toward neutral vehicles of information which tend to deal directly with the uncertainty. We all know that such consumer research organizations as Consumer Reports tend to promote informed consumer judgment, and we can reasonably surmise that reports of that kind, if generally circulated, would significantly limit the ability of advertising to enhance degrees of monopoly power, to say nothing of enabling consumers to spend their dollars more fruitfully.[15]

Similar demands to strengthen consumer education in Canada at the student and adult level have been made in this country, and such efforts deserve the fullest encouragement. Difficulties arise, however, when it comes to considering the practical implementation of proposals to strengthen consumer education in Canada. One question is: Where will the initiative and funds come from to finance consumer education?

The funds cannot come readily from private industry because of the possibility of suspicion of self-interest—though the possibility of setting up a private foundation should not be overlooked if adequate safeguards are provided for its complete independence and objectivity.

Governments, and that includes both the federal and provincial governments, would be the most obvious sources of financial assistance and encouragement, supplementing private funds raised by consumer organizations themselves. However, the difficulties in organizing and financing a strong consumer education movement need not deter Canadians from making serious efforts in this direction. The implications of the above discussion are presented in Chapter 18.

---

15 "Advertising and Competition", *op. cit.*, p. 6.

12

Costs

Does Advertising Raise Costs?

One of the main criticisms of advertising is that it adds to costs. These higher costs, initially borne by the businessman, are then passed on to the consumer resulting in the latter paying higher prices than might be necessary in the absence of advertising or if a reduction in advertising might be achieved. Advertising costs are added either at the producer level or the distributor level, or at both levels.

The final price effect—if not offset by increased productivity —may be greater if advertising costs are added at the producer level because distribution costs are frequently established on a percentage mark-up basis (including an allowance for profits) which has the effect of the distribution costs compounding the absolute amount of the mark-up since the latter is based on production costs *and* advertising costs.

To deal first with the argument that a good part of advertising costs is wasteful, and that some advertising does not provide any benefit to the consumer, the suggestion is that the wasteful part of advertising should be either eliminated or reduced through a variety of means, including possibly a tax on advertising and more rigorous administration of the provisions under the Combines Investigation Act.

Two general questions arise:

1. Do all advertising costs represent operating costs, or could some be regarded as growth costs?

2. Is wastefulness in advertising an isolated incidence or is waste generally a reflection of a wealthy nation that, if kept within reason, society can take in its stride?

On the first question, some of the advertising costs may be incurred in developing markets for new or improved products. There is a school of thought that holds that advertising expenditures of this kind should be regarded as growth costs like research expenditures and product development costs.

Professor Borden supports the view that "advertising and selling costs, particularly those devoted to new products and product differentiations, should be looked upon as growth costs, costs incurred by entrepreneurs in raising the level of economic activity."[1]

The implication of this type of reasoning is that society must incur certain basic costs if it is to continue to expand through the introduction of innovations and the making of capital expenditures (see Chapters 9 and 10).

A further point is that certain types of advertising expenditures fall into the category of essential efforts that must be pursued in modern society if the aggregate demand for goods and services is to grow at a rate adequate to keep pace with the expansion of the nation's productive capacity.

On the second question, Professor Johnson explains that a good deal of criticism against waste associated with advertising "derives much of its force from the assumption that our society

---

1 "The Economic Effects of Advertising", *op. cit.*, p. 266.

is poor, so poor that its ideal must be the utmost in austerity; in fact, our society is rich."[2]

Professor Johnson observes that a certain amount of waste is characteristic of a wealthy society and he concludes that "we can afford to buy advertised brands, instead of hunting for the lowest-priced source of supply. If we could not afford it, advertising would not exist, or at least the advertising that would exist would be so utilitarian as to be unobjectionable to even the most moralistic social critic."[3]

To turn now to two specific questions: Does advertising add to production costs? Does advertising add to distribution costs?

Advertising and Production Costs

Producers will advertise to obtain a market sufficient in size to allow them to sell the products they manufacture at prices which will enable them to recoup their costs and return a profit. As the market expands in size, it may be possible for the producer to achieve production economies. In that case, either some or all the costs of advertising may be offset by savings obtained through rising productivity as a result of larger-scale operations.

The industry studies undertaken by Professor Borden and referred to in Chapter 7 suggest that in some sectors advertising costs added to production costs, and in some sectors, they did not. Professor Borden concluded: "The answer to the question of advertising's effects on production costs is indeterminate."[4]

The question arises whether the fact that advertising may raise production costs for some products and for some industries, presents an adequate basis for criticism.

There are two aspects to the question. One is: Why do businessmen make the advertising expenditures in the first place? The answer presumably is—because without it they do not

---

2 *The Canadian Quandary, op. cit.,* p. 279.
3 *Ibid.*
4 "The Economic Effects of Advertising", *op. cit.,* p. 263.

expect to obtain access to a market large enough to ensure profitable production. Hence, what purpose is there to be served in considering accepting the suggestion that businessmen should eliminate or reduce advertising expenditures if they look at such expenditures as a factor to minimize risks and to maximize profits?

The other aspect to the question is: If businessmen could be persuaded to eliminate or reduce advertising, they would still be facing the problem they endeavoured to solve in the first place through advertising—the expansion or development of a market and consumer acceptance of their product. If they cannot advertise, they may turn to alternative methods of selling, personal selling and other promotional efforts that in the end may be more costly than the advertising expenditures contemplated in the first instance. It will be recalled that one of the main reasons for businessmen turning increasingly to advertising is that it is a more economic form of selling than other methods available. Would the social interest be best served if low-cost production and marketing methods were to be replaced by high-cost methods?

Advertising and Distribution Costs

The criticism that advertising costs add to distribution costs has not been so much against advertising *per se*—because even the most ardent critics of advertising admit that some of it represents an essential and economic service in marketing goods and services—but against unnecessary and excessive competition in advertising among distributors. Such inordinately high advertising costs, so it is claimed, do not necessarily increase the total sales of a particular commodity but rather affect its distribution among different suppliers. Professor Borden observes:

> In fields in which such intensive competition in advertising has existed, the use of advertising, like the use of other forms of non-price competition, has increased the costs of distribution, or at least has held these costs at high levels. In many of these instances, however, consumers have shown a willing-

ness to pay for the costs which attend the vigorously advertised products, for in large numbers they have not exercised the options open to them of buying lower-price, non-advertised merchandise. Instances of this kind were found in many fields, but especially clear were the instances in the dentifrice, cigarette, and grocery fields.[5]

Other conclusions reached by Professor Borden are:

1.   Advertising contributes to increasing the size of distribution companies. But such increases in operations do not necessarily mean lower distribution costs. In fact, distribution costs of some of the larger corporations rise as these companies grow in size. In some instances, however, a net gain may occur with increased selling costs being offset by a reduction in production costs achieved as a result of selling to a larger market.

2.   Advertising costs of distribution are frequently high in the initial phase of marketing. But whenever advertising builds up a ready demand for brand-name products, the costs of selling those products tend to decline at the distributor level. Examples mentioned by Professor Borden include brand-name products in cigarette and grocery production.

3.   Advertising costs which contribute to higher prices of brand-name products may lead to the increasing use of lower price private-brand products which benefit from the advertising carried out to promote the brand-name products. Thus, advertising may not bring lower prices of brand-name products. Instead it widens the choice of the consumer to select between a higher price brand-name product and a lower price private-brand product —bearing in mind that the latter product may not have come into existence, had not the brand-name product been promoted in the first instance.

In the end, the consumer benefits, even though prices of brand-name products may be higher because of advertising costs being added to the distribution costs of these products.

---

5 *Ibid.*, p. 261.

Balancing some of the benefits that result from advertising related to distribution against some of the disadvantages, such as excessive advertising competition, Professor Borden concludes that the results of the industry studies undertaken do not make it possible for him to answer the question, "whether advertising has tended to increase distribution costs as a whole."[6]

Professor Borden explains:

> The distribution cost picture is obscured by the fact that advertising and distribution cost data of business concerns relate to numerous combinations of products and of functional services and these combinations are subject to constant shifting. The overall effects of advertising on total distribution costs cannot be traced.[7]

The advertising profession goes one step further. There will be instances where advertising creates mass markets for certain products leading to lower prices for consumers. But where this is not the case, and advertising expenditures represent an added cost of distribution and hence contribute to higher prices, such higher priced products, according to the Institute of Canadian Advertising, "will be bought by consumers over the longer term only if the consumer judges such higher prices to be justified in terms of value received. These value judgments may involve better quality, greater convenience and satisfaction, improved packaging, saving of time, energy, etc. The consumer retains his freedom of choice: he may buy the older products which may be lower priced; or he may decide there is an advantage in buying the higher-priced newer or modified products. Product differentiation thus provides the consumer with multiple choices in different price ranges, adjusted to his pocketbook and preferences."[8] (For further discussion of the problems encountered in product differentiation, see Chapter 5.)

---

6 *Ibid.*, p. 262.
7 *Ibid.*
8 *Proceedings* of the Special Joint Committee of the Senate and House of Commons on Consumer Credit (Prices), December 13, 1966, pp. 2003 and 2004.

Advertising Cost Trends

Data reflecting cost increases of advertising collected on a systematic and continuing basis covering the major media on a comparable basis are not available in Canada. Occasionally advertising industry representatives compile such figures from a variety of sources, reflecting the limitations of comparability thus obtained.

One such effort lists the following increases in the cost of advertising in Canada in terms of "average rate" or "average cost" over the period 1962-1966:[9]

Television	28 per cent
Radio	16 per cent
Daily newspapers	12 per cent
Weekend publications	7 per cent
Consumer magazines	16 per cent
Outdoor: full showing	19 per cent

This is another aspect of the statistical gap that exists in the advertising field in Canada and that needs to be filled.

---

[9] "Rising Radio-Television Rates Still Earn Advertisers Lowest Cost-per-Thousand", by D. DeNike and D. Sutherland, *Canadian Broadcaster*, January 26, 1967, pp. 14 and 15.

13

Payment

Concept of Payment

In considering the question of how advertising is paid for, this study is concerned with the manner in which society pays for the cost of advertising and not how a business firm or an individual pays for the advertisement placed in a communication medium.

Two aspects of the manner of paying for advertising are considered here.

One is to make the distinction between gross and net costs, and then to establish how society pays for such gross costs and what some of the means are of keeping these costs to a socially acceptable level.

The other is to trace the effects of advertising on possible economies that can be achieved both in production and in distribution, and on the subsidies provided to communication media. This leads to a discussion of how large such subsidies may be in the United States, the United Kingdom and Canada, and what some of the consequences would be if, as a result of a reduction in total advertising expenditures, the subsidy contribution to communication media was correspondingly reduced.

To state the concepts briefly: gross costs are the sum total of advertising expenditures made by business, individuals, institutions and governments.

Net costs may be the difference between:

1.   Gross costs and savings resulting from efficiencies achieved.

2.   Gross costs and the reduction in selling costs, comparing lower-priced advertising costs with higher-priced other selling methods.

3.   Gross costs and the subsidies provided to communication media.

These concepts are elaborated further on. To examine first: How is advertising paid for through higher productivity or higher prices?

Paying Through Higher Productivity

Advertising involves a cost that has to be paid for. In the main there are two ways of paying for it.[1]

One way is through increasing productivity. To the extent that advertising increases the size of the market and enables a firm to achieve production economies, advertising may be paid for from the resulting productivity increase.

Productivity improvement may be sufficient to cover the cost of advertising, but in most instances entrepreneurs will endeavour to do better than that because they are in business to achieve a net gain and not just to recover costs. If they succeed, productivity increases will not only cover the costs of advertising but

---

[1] The above appraisal refers to advertising serving private business purposes and primarily addressed to the consumer. Public advertising is part of government operating expenditures and is thus paid for out of general revenues. These payments represent a social cost borne by the taxpayer and incurred presumably for his benefit. Similarly, a large part of institutional advertising is financed from funds obtained from government sources.

will also provide higher net revenues to the businessmen which they can use in one of several ways or a combination of ways: pay higher wages and salaries, pay higher rewards to management, pay higher dividends to investors and/or reduce prices to consumers.

Paying Through Higher Prices

Where advertising expenditures do not result in production and distribution economies, the costs of advertising are usually added to the final sales prices and are ultimately paid for by the consumer. Thus higher prices ensue.

The critics of advertising say: the reason for such higher prices is, in part, unnecessary advertising expenditures that are being added to costs and thus represent a social waste. In practice, however, the situation is more complex. One economist explained it in these terms:

> The flat statement that the consumer "pays for the advertising" ignores the fact that the situation is seldom as straightforward as that, and does not recognize the possibility that advertising may sometimes lead to economies in production in the long run. Similarly the statement that the basic products retailed under different brand names—detergents, cigarettes, gasoline—are "all the same" is seldom quite true. Slight physical differences are influential, in these cases, in attracting the attention and allegiance of consumers. But in any case, as we have noticed, the less material differences embodied in the presentation of the product, the design of the package, and the appeal used in the advertisements themselves are perfectly real, for marketing purposes, and it cannot be argued with any conviction that the total response of the consumer would be quite the same in their absence.[2]

The author then proceeds to say that this argument is not a case for advertising *per se* but an explanation of the positive contribution that advertising may make in a competitive situation. Most authors who accept the positive *net* contribution of

---

2 *Advertising, A New Approach, op. cit.*, p. 111.

advertising to economic progress and social welfare stress that it is the reduction or the prevention of competition that contributes more to rising prices than rising advertising costs.

Professor Borden explains this situation in these terms:

> The danger of too little price competition is, in effect, the danger frequently mentioned by critics, namely, waste in distribution attending the use of advertising. When competition is carried on to a large extent in advertising and other non-price forms, competitive waste may develop in that distribution costs become high or remain high. The point need not be developed further, for the conclusion is adequately reviewed above. In so far as advertising and selling costs incurred by a concern are more than offset by production economies which result from increased scale of operations, there can be no complaint that advertising and selling costs are high and lead to competitive waste. In certain product fields, however, where advertising and selling costs are high, there is no evidence that these high costs are offset by production economies of the concerns which incur them. The high costs persist because effective price competition has been prevented by the existence of other strong appeals which have affected consumers' valuations.[3]

If one follows this line of reasoning, increasing competition could bring prices down or at least keep them from rising as much as they otherwise might have done. To the extent then that advertising increases competition, say through product differentiation and brand-name product appeal, it creates the circumstances that give consumers the advantages that stem from competition: price, quality and service.

To the extent that advertising establishes a market for brand-name products, it paves the way for the product imitator to bring forward lower-priced products. Thus competition takes on many forms with the ultimate benefits accruing to the consumer.

---

[3] "The Economic Effects of Advertising," *op. cit.*, p. 283.

Competition Reduces Social Costs

The point then is: advertising may contribute either to reducing prices of products to consumers, or to raising prices. If prices are lowered, the consumer benefits directly.

If prices are raised, as a result in part of higher advertising costs needed to cater to new markets or to expand existing markets, then new opportunities are opened up for the product imitator. As he enters the market the consumer is now offered a new choice: to buy the higher-priced brand-name product or the lower-priced private-brand product.

Thus advertising has contributed in the absence of monopoly situations and collusion to increasing competition, with consequent benefits to the consumer. The subject of artificial restraint on competition is dealt with in Chapter 15.

In formulating policy alternatives, decision makers in the legislature and in the Government may wish to address themselves to the question: Is increased competition likely to bring to the consumer greater price and other social benefits than can be achieved through reducing advertising expenditures (through public regulation or through fiscal means), bearing in mind that a reduction in advertising may bring about a reduction in competition (see Chapter 16).

Social Net Cost of Advertising

The social cost of advertising may be measured in terms of the *net* cost to the economy. There are several aspects to such an assessment. To mention three:

1. If advertising expenditures result in expanding the market for certain goods and services, and if economies are achieved through mass production and mass marketing, with the result of greater efficiency passed on to the consumer in the form of lower prices, then the *net* cost to society is the difference between the gains in efficiency and the additional costs of advertising.

2. If advertising expenditures replace expenditures made for more traditional and more costly other selling methods (e.g. the door-to-door salesman), then the *net* cost to society is the difference between advertising expenditures and the costs of selling, employing techniques other than advertising.

3. If advertising expenditures serve to some extent to subsidize communication media, whether print or broadcasting, and if the continuation of the services provided by these media are considered socially desirable as in the case of newspapers, radio and television, then the social net cost to the nation is the difference between total advertising expenditures and the subsidies made available to communication media. "

Should such subsidies be eliminated, the services provided by the communication media would have to be considerably reduced or financed in some other way. One example would be government subsidies such as are being paid to the C.B.C. to cover about three-quarters of its operating costs, with the remaining one-quarter obtained from commercial revenues. Another example would be the imposition of special charges to the public to pay for the service, as is the case in the United Kingdom where owners of television sets pay an annual fee.

There are no measurements available in Canada of the net social costs of advertising along the lines outlined above; this is another area awaiting further research and investigation. Some enquiries—still incomplete in many respects—have been made in this field in the United States and the United Kingdom.

It was found, for example, that "a little more than one-half" of advertising expenditures made in the United States were "in effect a subsidy to the print and broadcasting media for the support of newsgathering, informational, and entertainment services. . . . Of this subsidy, about two-thirds goes to support the print media, and almost three-quarters of this amount goes to newspapers. About one-third of the total serves to support the broadcast media, and almost three-quarters of this amount goes to television."[4]

The British economist, Nicholas Kaldor, in a study covering the situation in the United Kingdom just prior to World War II, concluded that a little more than one-fifth of British advertising expenditures went for subsidy of newsgathering and informational media.[5] While comparable information is not available relating to the post-World War II situation in the United Kingdom, it is likely that the proportion of total advertising expenditures serving as a subsidy to information and entertainment media has risen significantly, partly because of the increasing reliance on advertising as a more economic means of reaching the consumer than traditional selling methods, and partly as a result of the introduction of such new media as television. Private television stations in the U.K. have been absorbing an increasing proportion of advertising expenditures, which has enabled them, in turn, to give the public a desirable alternative program service.

Canadian Net Cost

In Canada, the proportion of the social *net* cost of advertising may not be as high as is the case in the United States, a little more than one-half of total expenditures.

To mention three reasons:

1. When a Canadian reads an American newspaper or an American magazine, subsidized by an American advertiser, the Canadian does not contribute directly to the subsidy—though he may do so indirectly if the reading of an advertisement in the newspaper or the magazine induces him to purchase an American product or service. Hence, a Canadian going to Florida, if he is motivated primarily by an advertisement in

---

[4] *Some Comments on the Role of Advertising in the American Economy —A Plea for Revaluation, op. cit.,* p. 7.
[5] *Essays on Value and Distribution,* by Nicholas Kaldor, The Free Press of Glencoe, New York, 1960.

a U.S. publication, is making his modest contribution to sharing in the subsidy that helps to finance the information and entertainment industry in the United States.

2. When a Canadian views a television program on a U.S. channel, he has the benefit of a service without any financial cost to himself. This service is being paid for, at least in part, by the American consumer to the extent that he pays for the net social costs of the advertising expenditures made in the United States.

3. When a Canadian views a sponsored program on the C.B.C., he participates in part in the social costs involved in advertising. But the part is limited to about one-quarter of the total operating budget of the C.B.C. since the balance is financed through Government subsidies[6] (for which the individual pays indirectly through taxes, of course).

Allowing for the differences that appear to exist between the degree to which advertising expenditures subsidize Canadian and American communication media, the Canadian ratio may be between one-third and two-fifths of total expenditures, rather than the over one-half ratio indicated for the United States. Again, the Canadian range of ratios, assumed above, is subject to alteration in the light of quantitative evidence becoming available as a result of research work that may be undertaken.

But assuming that such a lower range of ratios is applicable to Canadian conditions, what is the extent of possible subsidization of information and entertainment media in Canada? In 1966, advertising expenditures (gross) were estimated at $821 million. Deducting advertising agency commissions of $55 million leaves net advertising expenditures of $766 million. The amount would be approximately equivalent to the commercial revenues received by communication media in Canada. Assuming that a one-third to two-fifths ratio is applicable to the Canadian

---

6 *Report* of the Committee on Broadcasting, *op. cit.*, p. 221.

situation, this suggests that between $250 million and $300 million spent on advertising in Canada represents a subsidy to information and entertainment media.

Implication of a Cut in Advertising on Communication Media

In the present stage of knowledge of the effect of advertising on economic activity in Canada, the figures mentioned above are only illustrative of the range of possibilities of the extent to which advertisers may be subsidizing communication media, in the sense that revenues received by the communication media from advertising make it possible for these media to render services which the public wants and which could not otherwise be supplied without compensating sources of income. But even the approximate character of the figures suggests that a great deal is at stake.

If the tax on advertising could be made really effective—and there appears to be a certain amount of doubt about the practicability of it (elaborated further in Chapter 16)—and if this cutback could be extended to cover the full subsidy that may presently be going to communication media, what would happen to Canadian newspapers, magazines, radio and television stations, including the C.B.C.?[7]

Could the communication industry take a one-third to two-fifths reduction in its advertising revenues in its stride without severe cutbacks in services, a number of bankruptcies and strong demands for government subsidies to replace private subsidies?

---

[7] Advertising experts claim that if, as the result of a tax on advertising, such expenditures were cut back by 20 per cent, the result would be: "About 30 per cent of the small newspapers in this country would go bankrupt ... (and) one-third of the stations other than the private network stations would be put out of business. . . ." [See statement by J. M. Milne, 1st Vice-President, The Institute of Canadian Advertising, *Proceedings* of the Special Joint Committee of the Senate and House of Commons on Consumer Credit (Prices), December 13, 1966, pp. 2019 and 2020.]

Need to Assess Total Effects

This exercise in quantifying for purpose of illustration some of the economic consequences of a cutback in advertising expenditures is not made with a view either to support a proposal for a tax on advertising by suggesting the potentialities of such a cutback, or to indicate the undesirability of the tax by illustrating some of the adverse effects of a tax on advertising on information and entertainment media.

Rather the purpose is twofold: One is to draw attention to the fact that little is known about the social net cost of advertising in Canada. The other is to point out how difficult it would be to make policy decisions on important matters of principle, such as a tax on advertising, without first examining the *total* effects of such a tax on all aspects of Canadian economic and social life, and that includes not only industry and the consumer, but also the communication media and the vital role they play in Canadian national, political and cultural development.

14

Inflation

Types of Inflation

Inflation may be of two kinds. One type is demand-pull inflation. This is a situation where the aggregate demand for goods and services exceeds the aggregate supply of goods and services available (after allowing for net imports of goods and services). Or, to use a popular phrase: "Too many dollars are chasing too few goods."

The other type is cost-push inflation. In this case, prices may increase as a result of production costs rising more rapidly than productivity, whether such increases in production costs are the result of higher wages, higher profits or higher interest rates, or a combination of all three. As business firms pass on these higher costs to consumers, higher prices ensue.

The claim has been made that advertising contributes to increasing the aggregate demand of goods and services. In a period of demand-pull type of inflation, the effect of advertising has been compared with "throwing gasoline on a fire that is already burning briskly".[1] The basic cause for rising prices in

---

[1] D. H. Fullerton, Evidence before the Special Joint Senate and House of Commons Committee on Consumer Credit (Prices), *Proceedings*, Queen's Printer, Ottawa, November 15, 1966, pp. 1294 ff.

136

such a period is the excess of aggregate demand for goods and services over the supply of such goods and services.

Advertising and Aggregate Demand

The question arises: In a period of inflationary pressures, is it advertising that contributes directly to raising aggregate demand for goods and services to a level in excess of the supply of such goods and services becoming available? Or does there exist another factor, more important than advertising, that contributes to such a situation? If so, what is this factor? Could it be higher incomes, rising at a rate substantially in excess of increasing productivity?[2]

Nicholas Kaldor takes a different approach. He distinguishes between the expansionist and the non-expansionist effect of advertising on the sales to consumers. He makes the point that advertising has a profound effect on the aggregate demand for certain classes of commodities such as "patent medicines, hair treatments, etc., or certain types of patent foods, like breakfast cereals or health beverages".[3] But for the large number of items which Professor Kaldor classed as "fundamental" types of commodities, he concluded that it was much more doubtful whether advertising has any significant effects on the *total* consumption of these goods.

In trying to deal with these questions, let it be said at the outset that inadequate factual evidence exists in Canada to demonstrate quantitatively the economic effects of advertising on aggregate demand for goods and services.[4] Hence, at this

---

[2] It bears emphasis that by singling out one factor for analysis, as above, the significance of many other factors contributing to inflation should not be overlooked. Such factors may include price pressures originating abroad and transmitted to the domestic economy through foreign trade, physical bottlenecks, inadequate labour mobility and strikes, government deficits and generally ineffective government economic policies, etc.

[3] *Essays on Value and Distribution, op. cit.,* p. 109.

[4] This is also true for the United States where a considerable amount of research work has been undertaken in assessing the economic impact of advertising on American society. The foremost contribution in this field is by Prof. Neil H. Borden of the Harvard Graduate

(Footnote continued on next page)

stage, only certain generalizations can be presented that are subject to verification in the light of results of further research that may be undertaken in the future.

Advertising Industry and Advertising Process

To begin with, it is necessary to make a distinction between the advertising industry and the advertising process.

The advertising industry comprises the people who draw their livelihood from the advertising expenditures made by business, institutions and governments. They are the people working in advertising agencies, communication media, and industry itself, and they include writers, artists, salesmen, clerks, technicians and executives. They are paid salaries and wages if they are employees, fees if they are professionals, and profits if they are entrepreneurs.

To the extent that advertising expenditures provide gainful occupation for these people and to the extent that persons working in the advertising industry spend part of their earnings on consumer goods and services, they add directly to the aggregate demand for goods and services in the country. There does not exist an adequate measure of how many people are employed in the advertising industry in Canada. But, subject to further investigations, it appears that only a fraction of one per cent of the labour force involves persons directly associated with the advertising business in Canada (excluding persons employed in government or business generally).

The advertising process, on the other hand, presents the means that communicate information about goods and services to consumers or tries to persuade consumers to buy a particular good or service.[5] It is "advertising" *per se* that is being claimed

---

School of Business Administration, dealing with "The Economic Effects of Advertising", referred to earlier.

[5] Again the analysis is presented in a simplified form. Reference is made to advertising addressed to the consumer. Thus industrial, institutional and government advertising is excluded.

to be the culprit if it performs a service contrary to the best interests of the consumer. The critics of advertising claim that this is the case in an inflationary period, since "most advertising is directed at persuading people to consume—not to save."[6]

The claim then is that in a period of inflation of the demand-pull type, advertising, by persuading people to buy more than they ordinarily would be prepared to do, contributes to inflation. How justified is this claim?

Social and Environmental Conditions

As stated previously, Professor Neil H. Borden has made an exhaustive study of the subject by examining the economic effects of advertising in a number of specific industries in the United States. Even though Professor Borden was unable to come up with a quantitative assessment of the overall effect of advertising on aggregate demand for goods and services, he was able to conclude on the basis of the special industry studies which he conducted, that demand for products was "determined primarily by underlying social and environmental conditions".

So that Professor Borden's findings can be understood in their context, the appropriate quotation is reproduced in full:

> Study of demand for a wide range of products leads to the conclusion that basic trends of demand for products are determined primarily by underlying social and environmental conditions, and that advertising by itself serves not so much to increase demand for a product as to speed up the expansion of a demand that would come from favouring conditions, or to retard adverse demand trends due to unfavourable conditions. The demands for some products, for example, lettuce, sugar, green vegetables, and professional services, have grown even though the products are little advertised, for underlying social and environmental conditions have been favourable to expansion

6 *Proceedings* of the Special Joint Committee of the Senate and House of Commons on Consumer Credit (Prices), November 15, 1966, pp. 1294 ff.

of their demand. Other industries for which there have been underlying conditions favourable to demand expansion have had their demand more rapidly expanded through use of advertising than would have occurred without such advertising. Among the products studied, this quickening of expansion has occurred in the case of cigarettes, dentifrices, oranges, automatic refrigerators, and other mechanical products such as automobiles, radios, and electric washers. On the other hand, for certain products for which underlying conditions caused adverse demand trends, demand was found to continue to contract in spite of considerable expenditures for advertising and promotion. Such was the situation with cigars, smoking tobacco, furniture, wheat flour, and men's shoes. In these instances advertising was powerless to reverse underlying declining trends, although it probably served to retard the declines. In other instances, certain products have had relatively constant per capita consumption over a period of years, even though substantial advertising was devoted to them. In short, such contrasting demand situations as mentioned above led to the conclusion that consumers' wants for products are determined by the character of consumers and their existing environment. Advertising has not changed people's characteristics; it has changed environment only as it has contributed indirectly over a long period in helping to bring a mobile society and a dynamic economy. In speeding up demand for new products it has contributed to the dynamic character of the economy.[7]

To return now to the question: Does advertising contribute directly to aggregate demand for goods and services? The answer is: Yes, as far as the fraction of one per cent of the labour force comprising persons directly employed in the advertising industry is concerned.

Income Affecting Demand for Goods and Services

As for the effect of the bulk of advertising expenditures that is made to inform and to persuade consumers, the situation is much less clear-cut.

---

[7] "The Economic Effects of Advertising", *op. cit.*, pp. 251 and 252.

If one accepts Professor Borden's thesis that it is primarily the "underlying social and environmental conditions" that affect aggregate demand for goods and services and not the messages that are carried to consumers as a result of advertising, then the question arises what economic factors may be responsible for translating wants created by "underlying social and environmental conditions" into actual demand for goods and services.

The most obvious answer is: rising income. For it is income increasing at a rapid rate that may encourage consumers to demand goods and services in quantities that may exceed the capacity of the economy to supply at a given point of time.

Advertising Affecting Income

Does advertising contribute directly to raising income? Using the term "advertising" in the sense of the advertising process, the answer is: No.

But this "no" must be qualified. For though the advertising process does not directly affect income, it facilitates the working of the economic system as it is now in operation in Canada and thus it makes an indirect contribution to raising income levels in the country, just as most other activities do that affect the economic life of the nation, from education to health, from government policy to business leadership, from export to domestic investment.

To trace some of the indirect contributions which advertising makes to raising income levels:

Advertising will inform consumers not only of the types of traditional goods and services available for sale, their quality, price, etc., but it will also bring to the attention of consumers new types or improved types of goods and services coming on the market.

By encouraging consumers to purchase such goods and services, advertising helps businessmen to determine the desirability of proceeding with the expansion of plant capacity, the purchase of new machinery and equipment, or the diversification and re-orientation of their operations. Based on the favourable assessment of market prospects, businessmen may then proceed to spend additional sums on expanded or improved or entirely new capital facilities.

Higher investment in turn is one of the most dynamic factors contributing to continuing economic growth, a rise in real Gross National Product, expanded levels of employment, improved earnings, higher standards of living and greater social welfare.

Higher levels of real income make it possible for income earners to spend more on consumer goods and services. Thus advertising, through encouraging businessmen to spend more on investment, is a factor that may contribute at times significantly to higher earnings in the country. Hence, higher earnings make it possible for income earners to spend more money on goods and services in the first instance than they would be able to spend in the absence of increases in earnings, and not increases in advertising.

Canadian Situation

Quantitative evidence to substantiate the above hypothesis awaits further research in the field of the economic implications of advertising. For the purpose of illustration, however, some references to recent trends may be helpful covering advertising expenditures, personal disposal of income, consumer spending and personal savings in Canada.

Table 3 presents data for the year 1961 to 1966, a period of continuing economic expansion including more latterly a period of price pressures. These data are set against Canadian postwar experience going back to 1946, with comments confined to the more recent period.

In 1966, personal disposable income in Canada was estimated at $38.3 billion, consumer expenditures at $34.9 billion and

Table 3

PERSONAL DISPOSABLE INCOME, CONSUMER EXPENDITURES AND
PERSONAL SAVINGS, CANADA, 1946-1966

Year	Personal Disposable Income[1] ($ millions)	Consumer Expenditures[2]		Personal Savings[3]	
		Total ($ millions)	Percentage of Personal Disposable Income	Total ($ millions)	Percentage of Personal Disposable Income
1946	8,923	8,031	90.0	892	10.0
1947	9,584	9,090	94.8	494	5.2
1948	11,079	10,085	91.0	994	9.0
1949	11,849	10,923	92.2	926	7.8
1950	12,688	12,026	94.8	662	5.2
1951	14,794	13,460	91.0	1,334	9.0
1952	16,072	14,781	92.0	1,291	8.0
1953	16,904	15,592	92.2	1,312	7.8
1954	16,984	16,175	95.2	809	4.8
1955	18,239	17,389	95.3	850	4.7
1956	20,153	18,833	93.5	1,320	6.5
1957	21,274	20,072	94.3	1,202	5.7
1958	22,880	21,245	92.9	1,635	7.1
1959	23,948	22,591	94.3	1,357	5.7
1960	25,075	23,540	93.9	1,535	6.1
1961	26,011	24,466	94.1	1,545	5.9
1962	28,243	25,926	91.8	2,317	8.2
1963	30,018	27,487	91.6	2,531	8.4
1964	31,725	29,666	93.5	2,059	6.5
1965	34,990	32,063	91.6	2,927	8.4
1966[4]	38,320	34,870	91.0	3,450	9.0
Percentage Increases					
1946-1951	65.8	67.6	—	49.6	—
1951-1956	36.2	39.9	—	–1.0	—
1956-1961	29.1	29.9	—	17.0	—
1961-1966	47.3	42.5	—	123.3	—
1946-1966	329.5	334.2	—	286.8	—

[1] This covers personal income less direct taxes.

[2] On goods and services.

[3] This is a net figure arrived at by deducting consumer expenditures on goods and services from personal disposable income; personal net savings include an allowance for changes in farm inventories.

[4] Preliminary estimates.

SOURCE: Data for 1946-1965 from *National Accounts, Income and Expenditure, 1965*, Dominion Bureau of Statistics, Ottawa, 1966, and earlier issues; data for 1966 are preliminary estimates based on partial data from *National Accounts, Income and Expenditure, Second Quarter, 1966*, Dominion Bureau of Statistics, Ottawa, 1966.

personal savings at $3.4 billion. Personal savings comprised 9 per cent of personal disposable income in that year.[8]

In 1961 the proportion which Canadians devoted to personal savings was about 6 per cent. As the data below show, personal savings increased at a considerably more rapid rate than personal disposable income, consumer expenditures or advertising expenditures[9] over the period 1961 to 1966.

	Percentage Increase
Personal disposable income	47
Consumer expenditures	43
Personal savings	123
Advertising expenditures	37

Does the fact that personal savings have more than doubled over the last five years while personal disposable income rose by close to one-half suggest that advertising has been a major factor in persuading the consumer to spend more than he was willing to do and to save less?

Does the fact that increases in consumer expenditures over the last five years amounted to 43 per cent, and in personal disposable income 47 per cent, as against a rise of 37 per cent for advertising expenditures suggest that advertisers have done such an outstanding job in persuading the consumers to spend more on goods and services than the proportion of his income which he was willing to devote for this purpose?

What the figures suggest, and again this hypothesis is subject to testing in the light of research, is that consumers, as Professor Borden suggests, are influenced by the social and environmental conditions of their day, as well as by their assessment of what is in their own best long-term interest, in dividing their earnings between what they wish to spend and what they wish to save.

---

8 The above estimates have been based on figures available for the first half of 1966. Revised estimates may yield a somewhat smaller ratio, but this ratio is not likely to be less than the 1965 ratio of 8.4 per cent, and it may well be higher.

9 Advertising addressed to the consumer may have risen more rapidly than total advertising expenditures (see Chapter 11).

Problem of Demand-Pull Inflation

If subsequent research tended to support this conclusion, it would throw an interesting light on the question of how to deal with inflation of the demand-pull variety. For if it is higher income that creates demand pressures in the first instance and not higher advertising, then the way to deal with the situation is to consider fiscal and monetary measures which aim at keeping disposable personal income in an approximate relationship with the expanding capacity of the country to produce goods and services, taking into account the increases in the balance of payments deficit that the economy is able to take into its stride.

If this is the most effective way of dealing with demand-pull type inflation, then there would be little support for a proposal that would be based on the expectation that the imposition of a tax on advertising would bring down prices in general.

Presumably, the most effective way of bringing down prices would be through measures designed to increase national productivity and to increase competition. To the extent that advertising contributes to increasing competition, it represents an important safeguard against prices rising as much as they would if competition were lessened (see also Chapters 15 and 16).

There is another aspect to this. Advertising contributes to consumer awareness of alternative choices in terms of quality and serviceability of products, and their prices. Hence, a well-informed consumer is likely to be more selective. To win him over may require greater efforts of persuasion on the part of business firms, and/or more sophisticated forms of advertising communications. Lower prices would represent real inducements, but these are likely to be brought about only through increasing competition.

To the extent that advertising contributes to increasing competition, it mitigates against prices rising as much as they would if competition were lessened. An example of competition contributing to lower prices even in the light of higher costs can be found in comparing food prices in major cities with those in towns and villages. A recent survey of food prices in Toronto and other metropolitan cities showed that in fact such prices were lower in these urban centres than in smaller towns. Two of the reasons given were: "highly competitive market because of several larger chain stores" and "better consumer knowledge because of extensive advertising."[10]

What in essence these surveys appear to imply is that increasing consumer knowledge, to which advertising of the informative type contributes, may be an anti-inflationary factor in a demand-pull type inflationary situation.

---

[10] *Proceedings* of the Special Joint Committee of the Senate and House of Commons on Consumer Credit (Prices), December 13, 1966, p. 1998.

15

Competition

Usefulness of Controversy

The effect that excessive advertising and certain advertising practices may have on concentration of industry, diminution of competition and price maintenance has been briefly referred to in Chapter 3, in discussing some of the disadvantages which critics of advertising claim are inherent in the system of advertising as it is presently practised in North America.

The literature on advertising and competition is as voluminous as it is controversial, but such controversy has a useful contribution to make to public debate.

It presents available evidence. It points to the gap in knowledge of the working of competition and the effect of advertising on it. It sharpens professional analysis of the subject, and refines legal interpretation.

It presents arguments for and against advertising, thus enabling the public and decision makers in the legislature and in Government to look at the problems involved from every point of view. It helps to crystallize the issues, thus paving the way to consider alternative solutions to the problems. And finally, it makes it possible to formulate rational decisions in the light of carefully considered evidence and arguments, representing all the interested parties concerned and taking into account the national interest.

Competition and Free Enterprise

To commence this discussion first with the classic explanation which Professor Chamberlain has offered about the relationship between competition and free enterprise. He states:

> "Free enterprise" has too long been loosely identified with "competition". In economic theory the identification has been with "perfect" or with "pure" competition. Yet it must be obvious that the typical outcome of free enterprise is not pure competition, but monopolistic competition. Commodities are differentiated partly by their very nature (without regard to demand), and partly in response to differences in buyers' tastes, preferences, locations, etc., which are as much a part of the order of things *within* any broad class of product as they are *between* one class of product and another. Heterogeneity from these causes is vastly increased by businessmen under "free enterprise", in their efforts further to distinguish their commodity from others and to manipulate the demand for it through advertising. In other words, an essential part of free enterprise is the attempt of every business man to build up his own monopoly, extending it wherever possible and defending it against the attempts of others to extend theirs. . . . "Freedom", in the sense of freedom from social control, may evidently lead also to agreements and to various forms of associative action between the individual economic units, whether firms or individuals. Such agreements are obviously monopolistic, and must clearly be added to the picture here given of the economic system as a blend of monopoly and competition. . . . The danger to be avoided is to conceive of the system as "competitive" in the absence of such agreements.[1]

One of the implications of what Professor Chamberlain has to say, as far as advertising is concerned, is that it represents

[1] *The Theory of Monopolistic Competition: A Re-orientation of the Theory of Value*, by Edward Hastings Chamberlin, Harvard University Press, Cambridge, Mass., 1962, pp. 213 and 214.

an aid to business to achieve product differentiation. The latter in turn is a means of increasing sales and profits, and "sales", Professor Chamberlain explains, "are a function of both price and advertising."[2]

Circular Flow of Competition

Professor Taplin deals with the relationship between competition and advertising by devoting a full chapter to the subject in his book *Advertising, A New Approach*. He explains the process at work as a circular flow of competition, with one competitor following another, each trying to outdo the other, only to be outdone by the next in the round following.[3] To quote:

> In our search for the best possible use to make of life and leisure we might not make such progress when left to ourselves as we may by means of the activities of advertisers in competition with each other. Wants become effective in economic action by being made progressively explicit. The advertiser, out to sell his goods, is continuously trying to "ring the bell" in the mind of the potential consumer. He may succeed, but then be displaced by another advertiser who rings it louder, by a more telling, and probably more accurate, appeal to the consumer's wants. So the first advertiser must try again. This is competition.[4]

Competition, Professor Taplin goes on to say, sharpens the search for latent wants. He observes:

> An advertiser in such a case is competing with other advertisers in presenting new schemes of wants to the consumer, and at the same time attempting to divert the attention of the consumer himself toward a new scheme of wants and away from the old one which he has already. In either case it can degenerate into a mere shouting match, a bid for attention as such, with the object to which attention is being directed playing a secondary role. Yet the possibility remains that in

---

[2] *Ibid.*, p. 300.

[3] Most of this write-up on competition is based on Chapter 5 of Professor Walter Taplin's book, *Advertising, A New Approach (op. cit.)* and the reader interested in the subject may find it rewarding to refer to this well-written book.

[4] *Ibid.*, p. 103.

the second manifestation, in which a new idea is pitted against the consumer's existing habits, some genuine progress may take place.[5]

Professor Taplin mentions other arguments in favour of competition, including the "pressure which it sets up toward economy in carrying out known operations, its tendency to make producers pass on to consumers the benefits of the economies they achieve, the reduction of individuals' dependence on a single supplier, and the claim that there is some attraction in competition as such which draws men of exceptional ability and keeps them on the job."[6]

Competition further stimulates consumers to re-examine "their consuming habits, presents them with an increasing range of choice, attracts good brains into production and gets the best out of them."[7]

Competition has its ills, and these may be magnified through advertising. Professor Taplin lists these:

1. Forcible imposition on consumers, such as advertising to captive audiences. An example would be broadcast advertising on American buses.

2. Limiting competition, which may be based, among other means, on "an understanding between the producers that nobody will offer to sell at a price below a certain acceptable minimum. . . . In combination with the kind of competitive advertising which is so expensive that the price *cannot* fall below a certain level, it produces a situation in which the consumer must accept both the advertising *and* the price, or go without."[8]

3. In an oligopoly situation where there are few sellers and where these virtually control all supplies among them, the sellers may decide "to compete with each other by means of advertising,

---

5 *Ibid.*, p. 104.
6 *Ibid.*
7 *Ibid.*, p. 105.
8 *Ibid.*, pp. 106 and 107.

and although the consumers object to this they are unable to have recourse to unadvertised alternatives, since these do not exist. Often the reason for the absence of these alternatives in a situation of oligopoly is the extremely heavy and expensive nature of the manufacturing plant employed, but when it is the necessarily large scale of the advertising itself which limits the possibilities of new entrants, a particularly vicious circle is set up."[9]

If such a situation arises, the consumer may resent it. He may not be happy about the interference with his personal freedom and he may feel that competitive advertising, if it reaches a certain level, or is of a certain kind, may be wasteful, costly, unnecessary and annoying.

In addition to the economic aspects of the effect of advertising on competition, so well explained in Professor Taplin's book, there are also certain legal aspects. These have been summarized recently in a symposium on "Advertising, Competition and the Antitrust Laws", organized by the American Bar Association in the United States. These legal aspects have been listed under the following headings (overlapping in part with economic and political aspects):

1. Potential mergers and acquisitions. In the light of developing case law, advertising and distribution patterns must be taken into account—but how?

2. Contacts among competitors. Horizontal cooperative advertising; agreements to limit advertising; and importantly, industry codes and enforcement.

3. Use and overuse of advertising as a predatory competitive weapon.

4. Congressional and executive rivalry to protect the consumer in this decade of politically popular consumer protection.[10]

---

9 *Ibid.*, p. 108.
10 "Advertising, Competition and the Antitrust Laws", Symposium sponsored by the Subcommittee on Regulations affecting Advertising

At the same conference, Richard B. Tennant presented an economist's point of view of advertising and its effect on competition and the American Anti-Trust Laws. His main points were: advertising *per se* is not anti-competitive, but excessive advertising may assist a firm or a group of firms in their efforts to restrain trade and thus may be a means of serving an unlawful purpose. Mr. Tennant offered these two main conclusions:

> First, advertising is not inherently anti-competitive, and therefore there is no place for an antitrust policy toward advertising in general. Advertising may, however, be a significant element in an anti-competitive situation and, as a part of a problem in restraint of trade and monopolization, may come into conflict with the law. Public antitrust policy toward advertising can properly be developed only in terms of the specific industrial situations in which such conflict occurs.

> Second, the development of policy therefore requires competent economic studies of industries where advertising is important and the proper and effective use of such studies in legal proceedings. Both the performance of the economic studies and their legal use are difficult tasks and the course of antitrust litigation to date (in other matters as well as advertising) gives little assurance that they will be well done.[11]

Mr. Tennant listed two areas in which advertising could get into conflict with the law. One was the area of "abuse", an infrequent occurrence. To quote:

> One possible area of contact between advertising and antitrust lies, of course, in the matter of abuse. Advertising is a lawful competitive weapon but like any other weapon may be used to excess or to some illegal end. An advertising campaign directed toward the exclusion of a smaller competitor by overwhelming him with vastly superior expenses, would be as unacceptable as a punitive price war to the same end. Alternatively, advertising might figure in a conspiracy to forego price competition and to limit competition to the less dangerous area

of the Committee on the Federal Trade Commission Act, Annual Meeting of the Section of Antitrust Law, American Bar Association, New York, August 10, 1964, pp. 158 and 159.

[11] "Advertising, Competition and the Antitrust Laws, An Economist's View," by Richard B. Tennant, *op. cit.*, p. 168.

of advertising. Or, it might be involved in a conspiracy to share markets by restricting advertising to particular geographical areas.[12]

The other area of possible conflict was the effect that advertising, if used in a certain manner and in large concentration, could have in affecting competition in a given industry. An example would be if advertising competition were used to the exclusion of price competition. Under such circumstances, Mr. Tennant explained, it was not the inherent anti-competitive aspect of advertising that was at issue but the fact that it became "part of a mix of influences that result in an industry structure or behaviour" considered to be not in the public interest.[13] Mr. Tennant explained:

> The major contact between advertising and antitrust to date and the major opportunities for a confrontation in the future lie in the legally less clear area of the role of advertising in competition. Advertising is one method of appealing to a market—highly effective for some kinds of products or services, less effective, or even useless, in the case of others. In those industries where it is most effective, like cigarettes or soap or some other low-value, high-volume consumers' goods, advertising may have an important effect on the structure of the industry and may constitute a significant aspect of its behaviour. If such structure or behaviour is in violation of existing law, or condemned by public policy as it develops in the future, then advertising might itself be illegal under a rule of reason or its control might offer a means of reform even if the illegality arises from some other source.[14]

Competitive Advertising

Professor Taplin lists these arguments in favour of competitive advertising:

1. "High production, and the full employment of an expensive plant, can in many cases be achieved and maintained only

---

12 *Ibid.*, p. 169.
13 *Ibid.*, p. 170.
14 *Ibid.*, p. 169.

by extensive use of advertising, the alternative being to produce on a smaller scale, and at a higher cost per unit, without advertising. This argument is sometimes true and sometimes not, according to the particular circumstances of the case."[15]

2. Competitive advertising reduces risk and thus represents "a form of insurance against the possibility of insufficient demand for their products."[16] The achievement of this objective may be greatly aided through market research which is increasingly becoming more sophisticated and widespread.

3. Competitive advertising assists in the development of human wants and in their transformation into effective demand for goods and services, which, in turn, means a pushing back of the "frontiers of demand".[17]

4. Competitive advertising performs a constructive service to society at a price. The question is: Is the price too high? Professor Taplin answers this question:

> We can say that the existence of competition between those agents who offer advertising services to those who have something to sell, and the tendency of businessmen to buy those services at the lowest figure consistent with their proper performance, should help to keep the price down. But to argue that greater satisfaction would result from the expenditure of the money on services other than advertising (which is a rather devious way of saying that the price of advertising is too high) is to become entangled in the terminology of what is called "welfare economics".[18]

But in the end, according to Professor Taplin, "the argument against competitive advertising only stands if (1) it is genuinely a matter of complete indifference to the consumer whether he buys one brand or another, and (2) no genuine market test by price is available, which means, in effect, that there is no unadvertised alternative. These conditions are very rarely satisfied.

---

15 *Advertising, A New Approach, op. cit.,* p. 112.
16 *Ibid.,* p. 114.
17 *Ibid.,* p. 117.
18 *Ibid.,* p. 118.

But when they are, there is a *prima facie* case against competitive advertising, and the situation is obviously worse when it comes about by collusion in keeping up prices."[19]

Price Competition

If competition in advertising brings both positive results and adverse effects, why not replace it by another type of competition—price competition which may bring the greatest benefits to consumers. The question may be asked: Why not reduce or eliminate "unnecessary" advertising and bring down prices? Professor Taplin replies:

> The question whether it pays a manufacturer to reduce prices or not depends in the first place on the elasticity of demand—whether a price change will produce a more or less proportionate increase or decrease in sales. This in turn has to be kept in relation to the manufacturer's own cost structure, in which various levels of sales will be associated with various levels of cost per unit. Clearly the elasticity of demand for particular brands is difficult to estimate in advance and in the absence of special circumstances or knowledge it appears just as likely that a manufacturer will pitch his price too low as that he will pitch it too high.
>
> The sort of special factors which may work against a price reduction are fairly obvious. Costs of production may be rigid or may even increase per unit of output when sales increase. Experience may have shown that demand is inelastic so that the manufacturer would gain little or nothing by lowering his price. In the case of oligopoly, sellers who have been to some degree insulated from the need to adjust prices to demand may decide not to lower them even when demand is known to be inelastic. Or there may be a general upward movement of the price level, which will reduce if not entirely offset the inducement to price reduction on the sales of a particular brand. And it may be that there is some more or less rational resistance on the part of the manufacturer to the risk of reducing his price, which he may judge to be greater than the risk of maintaining it at its present level or increasing it.[20]

19 *Ibid.*, p. 119.
20 *Ibid.*, p. 121.

Non-Price Competition

Professor Taplin presents his analysis of the effects of competitive advertising by saying that there is another alternative to it besides price competition, and that is non-price competition. An example of the latter would be promotional campaigns, such as premium offers, free samples, etc.

The use of promotional devices has become a more popular selling technique in recent years. As has been mentioned before, it represents, according to Professor Taplin, price competition in disguise. For the consumer gets something "extra", for which he is paying either in the form of a higher price for the product to which the premium was added, or by paying the same price with the premium representing the value of a possible reduction in price, which the seller might have been able to make, had he not given away a premium.

While in theory, alternatives exist between advertising competition, price competition and non-price competition, in actuality all three types of competition are closely interrelated. The emphasis on each specific type may change from time to time, from industry to industry, from firm to firm, depending on market conditions for specific commodities, expectations of entrepreneurs and the general state of the economy.

Thus, as far as non-price competition is concerned, this type of competition will continue to exist, as long as it finds acceptance among consumers and brings results to businessmen in the form of increased sales and profits.

Advertising Agencies and Communication Media
—Views on Competition

When the question, "Does advertising reduce competition?" is put to professional advertising executives, they find it difficult to conceive of a situation where this in fact would apply. For, "they live in a world of intensive and constant thrust and counterthrust —of endless study of the continuously dissatisfied consumer—of the most minute analyzing of their own and their competitors' every attempt to woo and win—always trying, as their competitors are, to get some little edge, however slight. To pause in the heat of this battle and even consider that all of this feverish effort could be related to *less* or *lessening* competition is, to them, quite inconceivable."[21]

These views, expressed by one of the leading advertising executives in the United States, are typical of the thinking in the advertising industry. To professionals in the industry, advertising means more competition, not less.

There are two other reasons why professional advertisers— and the communication media for that matter—can be expected to support competition in a free society.

The first is that business firms spend increasing sums of money on advertising to remain competitive. If competition were lessened, whether this was the result of a monopoly or oligopoly situation, or the consequence of a special combine, then the incentive to advertise might diminish. Hence, it is in the very self-interest of the advertising industry—and that includes the advertising agencies and the communication media— to support competition as strongly as possible, if not on grounds of principle, then on the grounds that their livelihood depends on it.

The second is that the basic job performed by the advertising industry is to find a customer, not to sell a product. The latter task is that of the producer or the distributor of the item involved. Hence, the principle of division of labour removes the advertising industry from the direct battle-line of competition for the consumer dollar. Their job is done if they have interested a potential consumer in the product advertised. Whether the sale

---

[21] "The View from the Market Place", by Henry M. Schachte, Executive Vice President, J. Walter Thompson Company, Paper given at the Symposium sponsored by the Subcommittee on Regulations affecting Advertising of the Committee on the Federal Trade Commission Act, Annual Meeting of the Section of Antitrust Law, American Bar Association, New York, August 10, 1964, p. 160.

is made, at what price, in a "perfect" or "imperfect" market (of which there are many and different kinds), this is a matter of prime concern to the producer and the distributor.

This is not to say that advertising agencies—and probably in the future communication media to an increasing extent—are not interested in what their clients are doing and how successful they are. This interest is in fact an essential part of the professional advertising executive's job. But this interest is not his prime responsibility because, if it were, he might as well run the company whose product he is trying to promote. His job is to serve his client as well as he knows how, without trying to do his client's job. The advertising executive's main task is to concentrate on advertising (and that includes research, market surveys, planning, etc.) and not on producing and distributing the products advertised.

This brief excursion in assessing the interests of advertising agencies and communication media in the subject of competition, and how it may be affected by advertising, is designed to illustrate the point that it would be an over-simplification of reality and of the diverse interests represented in the advertising process, to say that if advertising contributes, in certain situations, to a possible restraint of trade, everyone connected with it must share the blame.

Each case will require to be examined on its merits or demerits. Final judgment can then be made on proof of action contrary to the national interest, and not on association with a cause.

16

Tax

Justification for a Tax on Advertising

A tax on advertising may be justified on several grounds. To name four:

1. That some of the advertising expenditures are either wasteful and/or excessive. For example, the Royal Commission on Health Services recommended "that in the application of the provisions of the Corporation Income Tax Act to manufacturers, importers, and distributors of drugs, consideration should be given to establishing a maximum of 15% of total sales as the allowable deductible expense for advertising, sales promotion, 'detail man', and other similar items."[1]

2. That advertising revenues originating in Canada should be used primarily for the purpose of supporting Canadian publications and other communication media. For example, new legislative provisions in effect since January 1, 1966, provide that advertisers in Canada cannot claim income tax deductions for advertising placed in foreign publications aimed at the Canadian market. Canadian editions of foreign publications which have

---

[1] *Report* of the Royal Commission on Health Services, *op. cit.* p. 42.

been edited, printed and published in Canada at least since spring, 1964 are exempt (and these include the Canadian editions of *Time* and *Reader's Digest*).

3. That advertising contributes to inflation and that a tax on specific types of advertising would reduce pressures on limited supplies and prices. Such a proposal was made to the Special Joint Senate-House of Commons Committee on Consumer Credit (Prices) on November 15, 1966.[2]

4. That a tax on advertising would raise government revenues. While such proposals have so far not received much consideration in Canadian public discussion, taxes on revenues from advertising are in effect in other countries. One example is the United Kingdom, where commercial advertising on television stations is subject to a rather substantial tax since 1961.

Thus, taxes on advertising, not counting the war years when advertising was subject to special controls, is not an entirely new subject in Canada. Examples of such taxes in existence in a limited area in Canada today have been mentioned above. New voices are added from time to time suggesting their extension.

Perhaps one of the strongest criticisms of "excessive" advertising from an official body has come from the Royal Commission on Health Services, which after three years of investigation and on the basis of evidence obtained came to this conclusion, "that a good part of promotional effort in the drug industry is wasteful".[3]

Even the staunchest supporters of the advertising business would not wish to claim that all advertising serves constructive purposes and that there is no inefficiency, waste or mistaken judgment in carrying on advertising in Canada.

---

[2] See *Proceedings* of the Special Joint Committee of the Senate and House of Commons on Consumer Credit (Prices), November 15, 1966, pp. 1294 ff.

[3] *Report, op. cit.*, p. 666.

Nor could it be denied that Canadian publications fighting for their survival against overwhelming American competition would face a slow but continuing process of elimination and that it is in Canada's national interest to maintain a viable publication industry in this country.

Nor could it be said that there does not exist a substantial body of public opinion which holds that unnecessary advertising and excessive promotion may represent a significant factor in contributing to higher prices of consumer goods and services in Canada.

Nor could it be argued that taxes on communication media or placed directly on advertising would not bring added government revenue. The question involved would be more one of equitableness and fiscal soundness in deciding whether a tax on advertising or some other tax would best serve the national interest in a given situation.

Objections to a Tax on Advertising

The question that the assessment below is addressed to is this: Would it make economic sense to impose a tax on advertising, at least for a limited time, to combat inflation of the demand-pull type? Thus the discussion is limited to one aspect only of the broader area of the merits or demerits of taxing advertising in Canada.

Most objections against a tax on advertising are made on general grounds—that is, quite apart from the objections in principle that some people have against any increase in taxes—that it would affect adversely economic progress and reduce individual initiative, a prime motivating force in the growth process of most countries.

The following is an example of this type of objection:

> A restriction or tax on advertising must be a restriction or tax on initiative and on development. If we need more consumption then we must not inhibit the initiatives or the in-

vestment in securing it. The industrialists may surely be left to decide for themselves what initiatives and what volume of activity are compatible with running a sound business.[4]

But this general objection is too blunt a treatment of the merits or lack of merits of a proposal to impose a tax on advertising as a means of fighting inflation. A more subtle approach is the one presented by Walter Taplin, a research professor in Advertising and Promotional Activity at the London School of Economics. This author tries to put proposals for the tax on advertising in perspective by raising the question whether such a tax would be in the best interest of the consumer, for it is the consumer who wants lower prices. The author concludes that a tax on advertising is not likely to result in lower consumer prices. To quote:

> We should also take note of proposals for limiting the discretion of advertisers in spending money by taking it away from them in taxation. This is by no means a vague alternative in the minds of advertising men and others, for instance in the newspaper world, whose living depends on advertising revenue. To them it has all the terrifying clarity of a nightmare. How does it stand, as against other alternatives to expenditure on advertising, from the consumer's point of view? What the consumer likes, within reason and without slumps, is price competition. So what is that same consumer going to say to a new alternative which is *neither* competitive advertising at its present level *nor* price cuts, but less advertising without a reduction in prices but with more taxation? It is conceivable that the consumer may not like it even though he is given assurances that the State will spend the money more wisely than industry or the consumers could have done, or that the institution of this new tax *might* lead to the reduction of the old ones.
>
> This argument naturally does not exhaust the discussion of the whole question of the taxation of advertising. To do that we should have to consider whether such taxation would enable freedom, range and variety of choice by consumers to be maintained, how the introduction of new products would be affected, and how a tax on advertisements would compare, in the light of the normal tests of the efficiency of taxes, with

---

4 *The Influence and Techniques of Modern Advertising, op. cit.,* p. 5.

available alternatives. What the preceding argument attempts to do is to put taxation in its place as one of a large number of conceivable alternatives.[5]

The Institute of Canadian Advertising, appearing before a Parliamentary committee, emphasized the anti-inflationary character of advertising, and it raised the question: Why curb advertising if it contributes to the objective of keeping prices from rising unduly in a period of inflationary pressures? To quote:

> In many cases advertising, by contributing to the expansion of existing markets or the development of new ones, also contributes to lower prices and in such instances is anti-inflationary.

> Advertising also frequently lowers selling costs and in this regard also has an anti-inflationary influence.

> The consistent effort to make advertising dollars more effective is itself anti-inflationary.[6]

Without considerable study of the feasibility of the tax on advertising, its practicability, its effectiveness, its equitability, its administrative problems and the availability of other fiscal alternatives, it is difficult to offer more than some general comments. And even these must remain tentative, subject to further examination and reassessment in the light of new evidence and research work that may have a bearing on the issues involved.

Subject to these qualifications, the following broad generalizations may be brought forward.

In Chapter 15, the point was made, among others, that under the circumstances which confront most of Canada's industry, advertising facilitates competition. The latter provides consumers with the opportunities to choose the best products available at the price most acceptable to them.

---

5 *Advertising, A New Approach, op. cit.,* pp. 124 and 125.
6 *Proceedings* of the Special Joint Committee of the Senate and House of Commons on Consumer Credit (Prices), December 13, 1966, p. 2010.

Without competition, prices of goods and services sold would be higher, a fact that has been amply demonstrated in Canadian economic experience. Thus the maintenance of competition has become one of the basic objectives of government economic policy and various means have been and continue to be employed to achieve this objective including combines legislation, tariff policy, fiscal and credit measures, etc.

The point has been made previously, but it bears repeating that advertising is a means through which business firms inform the potential purchaser of the quality, serviceability and price of the product they offer for sale. Thus advertising becomes one of the most direct ways of one firm competing with another firm for a share of the consumer dollar, and it is one of the most economic means of achieving this objective.

Now, if a tax were imposed, designed to reduce advertising which serves to inform the consumer about the choices he has in buying goods and services, one of the important means of making competition more effective in a largely free enterprise and market-oriented economy would be interfered with.

The advocates of a tax on advertising could reply that such a tax should be imposed on advertising that endeavours to persuade consumers to buy and not on advertising that informs consumers.

This is a fine point indeed. But, in practice, most advertisements addressed to consumers which are designed to persuade consumers to buy, endeavour to do so by telling the consumer about the goods and services available for sale, their uses, prices, etc. Thus the "informative" aspect of advertising is inextricably intertwined with the "persuasive" aspect of advertising.

Assuming then that a reduction in advertising expenditures would lead to some lessening in competition, even though its extent may be difficult to measure, what would be some of the effects on prices?

Business firms would find that in a less competitive situation they could pass on cost increases to consumers in the form of higher prices. The consumer, being less adequately informed of the choices he may have in buying in the cheapest market, would have to pay these higher prices if he wanted to purchase such goods.

Business firms, knowing that they could pass on higher prices to the consumer because of lessened competition, would be less prone to continue to search for economies and push hard for productivity increases. Thus basic production costs would rise. The ultimate price paid by the consumer would be considerably higher because of the snowball effect of the price-setting system which provides for mark-up upon mark-up, as a commodity moves from the manufacturer to the wholesaler, then to the retailer, and finally to the consumer.

Hence in a situation when cost-push pressures are a major factor in raising prices, such as has been the Canadian experience in the more recent period and as appears to be the outlook for the near term, a reduction in advertising could lead to a lessening in competition. The latter could mean higher prices for two reasons:

First, because of lessened competition it would be less necessary for business to offer to the consumer goods and services at the lowest possible price. And secondly, management may find it less necessary to object to undue increases in production costs, knowing that because of lessened competition it could pass on such higher costs to the consumer.

From the consumer's point of view, what matters is whether a reduction in advertising will lead to lower prices. The claim is made that business firms would not likely reduce prices even if they cut their advertising costs somewhat in the light of a tax imposed on advertising. Various reasons are given. Funds becoming available from a reduction in advertising may be transferred to other promotional efforts. There may be need to offset other increases in production costs. Or profits which have been squeezed as a result of rising costs may have to be restored to earlier levels.

Such an unwillingness to pass on lower advertising costs to the consumer in the form of lower prices could be explained by the realization of business of not finding it necessary to reduce prices if competition is lessened.

On this point, the Institute of Canadian Advertising observed: "There is a distinct possibility that a tax on advertising would be passed on to the consumer in the form of higher prices whether or not advertising was reduced. Quite apart from the disruptive effects this may have on business generally in Canada, it would reduce competition. Lessened competition in turn would drive up prices. Canadians have found that they have been able to make tremendous economic progress and obtain the second highest standard of living in the world because of increased competition. Why curb progress?"[7]

Quite apart from the psychology of business firms in formulating price policies, what matters from an economic point of view is whether the reduction in advertising costs represents a real gain or whether there are offsetting disadvantages. While it cannot be said categorically at what point a reduction in advertising could exceed rising prices due to lessened competition, thus presenting a *net* gain to the consumer and passed on to him in the form of lower prices, past experience shows that the greatest gains made in North America from the consumer's point of view have been the result of increasing competition and not the result of a reduction in advertising.

In fact, as the data presented in Chapter 10 show, advertising expenditures in Canada and the United States have risen more slowly in the last five years of rapid economic expansion than Gross National Product and business investment. Similarly, personal disposable income and consumer expenditures in Canada

---

[7] *Ibid.*

have risen at a considerably greater rate during the period 1961 to 1966 than have advertising expenditures (see Chapter 14).

Balance of Payments Implications

This assessment of the impact of lessened competition on consumer prices has so far been limited to a discussion of the domestic situation, assuming a closed economy. But in fact Canada is an open economy. It is one of the largest trading nations of the world, with about two-thirds of its trade being carried on with the United States.

What would be the impact of foreign competition on Canadian industry should Canadian producers and distributors be subjected to a tax on advertising?

If domestic industry allowed its costs to creep up under the circumstances described above, it may find that it is pricing itself out of the Canadian market, not to speak of markets abroad where competition is usually much keener because Canadian manufacturers have to overcome foreign tariff barriers while in Canada they may enjoy certain tariff protection.

Advertising helps the Canadian producer to obtain access to the bulk of the Canadian market. It could be argued that the tax on advertising, leading to a reduction of advertising expenditures made by Canadian manufacturers and distributors, would have the same effect on advertising expenditures made by foreign suppliers, whether they sell goods produced in Canada (through foreign controlled subsidiaries) or whether they sell goods imported from abroad.

The bulk of imported goods comes from the United States. Canadians read American newspapers and magazines. Many of them listen to American radio stations and view American television programs, available to them directly from American television stations. The majority of Canadians live in sufficiently close proximity to the border with the United States to be able to tune in directly to American programs and thus be exposed to American commercials without using Canadian communication media.

Hence the importer of a commodity from the United States would be enjoying the full benefits of continuing advertising while the Canadian manufacturer and distributor, having been forced to cut back advertising because of a tax on advertising, would find it increasingly difficult to compete against the foreign supplier.

The result would be a change in the competitive pattern of doing business in Canada.

The competitive position of the domestic producer would be weakened. The competitive position of the importer would be strengthened.

A tax on advertising might hit small companies and Canadian owned corporations particularly hard, the former because there is a point where a reduction in advertising expenditures diminishes disproportionately the effectiveness of such advertising and the latter because of the adverse discriminatory treatment vis-à-vis foreign controlled companies. The adverse effects of a tax on advertising on Canadian owned corporations has been summarized in these terms:

> A tax on advertising might also make things especially rough on Canadian-owned companies in the consumer-products field. Companies with U.S. parents could utilize television from border cities like Detroit and Buffalo to reach a big chunk of the Canadian market with tax-free advertising; Canadian subsidiaries could reimburse their U.S. parents in a variety of ways. Meanwhile, Canadian firms with no U.S. affiliates to place advertising in this way would have to cut their advertising or spend more to maintain the present volume.[8]

In 1965 Canada had a balance of payments deficit with the United States of $1.9 billion and a total balance of payments deficit with all other countries of $1.1 billion. If the competitive

---

[8] "The Tax", by James Nuttall, *Sales/Promotion*, January 1967, p. 8.

position of Canadian producers were weakened by deliberate fiscal policy action on the part of the Canadian Government, without corresponding curtailment of foreign competition—and the latter could not be easily achieved since the majority of Canadians do not appear to support a policy which would interfere with the free flow of ideas and communications—then Canada's balance of payments deficit with the United States would rise further and so would the overall balance of payments deficit.

Would this be in Canada's long-term national interest?

Employment Implications

Adverse balance of payments repercussions of a tax on advertising would not only affect the value of the Canadian dollar and Canada's foreign exchange stability. It would also affect employment in this country. Increased imports would replace Canadian production, and this would mean fewer jobs in Canadian manufacturing industries and in the distributive trades and service occupations who depend for their livelihood on a prosperous Canadian manufacturing industry.

As employees were laid off in Canadian industries as a result of increased import competition, and to the extent that these people would not find jobs in other industries, this would affect adversely the ability of persons thus unemployed to continue to maintain their ordinary level of consumer spending. Hence, a primary lay-off in manufacturing industries would, through the multiplier effect, affect adversely the economy as a whole, bringing increases in unemployment and a slow-down in economic growth.

At a time when Canada's labour force is expanding at one of the most rapid rates in Canada's peace-time history, would it be in this country's best interest to pursue economic policies which reduce domestic employment opportunities and increase employment in other countries?

This is not to say that a tax on advertising would inevitably bring all the dire consequences of rising unemployment and increases in the balance of payments deficit mentioned above. There may be off-setting economic forces at work which may disguise the full effect of a tax on advertising. But some undesirable consequences are likely.

Are these wanted, whether they take the form of depriving some Canadians of their jobs, weakening the Canadian dollar or affecting adversely the confidence of the international community in Canada's ability to manage her economic affairs efficiently and equitably?

Temporary Expedient

Proponents of a tax on advertising, whether on all advertising or on selected types, may argue—though they may be required to produce stronger evidence than has been made available so far in support of the soundness of the proposal—that the proposed tax would not bring the adverse results listed below under seven headings:

1. Domestic competition would not be reduced.
2. Domestic production and distribution costs would not rise.
3. Domestic price pressures would not increase as a result of cost-push pressures.
4. Canada's balance of payments would not be adversely affected.
5. International confidence in Canada's ability to manage her own affairs rationally and effectively would not be undermined.
6. Ability of Canadian business to hold its own against foreign competition would not be reduced.
7. Unemployment in Canada would not rise.

Proponents of a tax on advertising could further argue: "Let us introduce a tax on a temporary basis and if any or all the adverse effects listed above materialize, and they are not out-weighed by other social benefits, then let us reverse the tax".

But such a proposal overlooks one basic fact of economic reality.

The competitive position of Canadian industry is too valuable an accomplishment, achieved as a result of a struggle over a century, to be trifled with temporary expedients that may bring results contrary to what the measures were designed to achieve.

An "on" and "off" tax on advertising, tied to variations in the business cycle—on in boom times and off in a recession—would be like using the tariff system to give industry protection in periods of declining sales and removing or reducing that pro-tection when sales rose and the economy prospered. This idea of raising tariffs in "bad" times and reducing them in "good" times —that is, changes in tariff policy in the light of variations in the business cycle—are reminiscent of the "beggar-thy-neighbour" trade and foreign exchange policies pursued by nations in the depressed thirties and long discarded since.

The following comments are illustrative of some of the difficul-ties that may be created if a tax on advertising were to be used as a specific anti-cyclical fiscal instrument:

> By the time the suggestion (tax on advertising) could be effectively implemented—considering long-term contracts, the long-range intent of most brand advertising, and the carry-over effect of previous advertising—the economic situation itself might well have moved into a new phase. Unfortunately, it would not then be possible to utilize advertising to support a rapid turn-around in sales, because national advertising does not work that quickly.[9]

Quite apart from the administrative difficulties of a tax on advertising, which, if designed to curb certain expenditures and not others, could be considered discriminatory, there is also need

---

9 *Proceedings* of the Special Joint Committee of the Senate and House of Commons on Consumer Credit (Prices), December 13, 1966, p. 2008.

to take into account the possible retroactive features of the fiscal policy device proposed.

Business firms plan ahead several years in developing new products. Similarly, it takes time and effort to plan and build new plants and to get into new production. If, in the meantime, Government imposes a tax on advertising, then the marketing of the new products—as well as many old products—may be adversely affected.

For the entrepreneur who has gone ahead and has built a new plant or bought new equipment cannot easily cancel or alter such expansion plans. If his contractual obligations or his investment are such that he cannot reverse his decision to proceed then he has only these alternatives: he can either proceed with his advertising campaign as planned and pass on the higher cost of advertising to the consumer in the form of higher prices,[10] or he can cut advertising and take his chances in marketing his products. In the former case, consumer prices would be higher; in the latter case, they are not likely to be lower because the risk of business succeeding has been increased with the reduction in advertising. Whenever a risk increases, business firms endeavour to allow for such a contingency.

Of the two possibilities mentioned above, which is the more likely? Most business firms would not wish to take chances in marketing new products after they had spent considerable sums on product research and development and on capital investment. Hence they are more likely to choose the course of proceeding with their advertising program as planned and passing on higher advertising costs—to the extent of the tax imposed—to consumers.

Another economic implication of a tax on advertising is the "lag" factor. Business firms plan advertising budgets for a period

---

[10] This assumes that business firms have done all they can to achieve economies and increase productivity so that there does not exist an opportunity of absorbing higher advertising costs through savings in other areas.

ahead, frequently for a year, sometimes less, sometimes longer. Contracts are entered into and other arrangements are made to implement the advertising plans. Quite apart from the legal complexities that may be caused and the business disruption that may ensue, from an economic point of view the "lag" factor may bring adverse results which advocates of a tax on advertising may not have had in mind in proposing it.

Advertising budgets are formulated by business firms to serve a purpose, say the marketing of a given volume of products for the coming year. If these firms were to reduce their advertising expenditures in response to a tax imposed on advertising in a period of inflation when market prospects were favourable, what would induce them to increase advertising expenditures in a period of declining economic activity or of slow growth when market prospects were less favourable, even though the Government may remove the tax on advertising at that time?

The experience appears to be that once business firms reduce expenditures of various types, whether for advertising or for other purposes, as a result of Government action or for other necessary reasons, they may be hesitant to reinstate such expenditures until there appears to be strong justification for doing so at some future date.

Thus the "lag" factor may aggravate a situation when Canada moves from the crest of a boom period to a period of slow growth. And the adverse effects could become cumulative should a recession threaten.

Thus fiscal policy devices that have a "lag" factor of long duration are less desirable instruments to cope with short-term economic problems including cyclical variations than are measures that bring results reasonably quickly and that do not have undesirable after-effects of long duration.

In this connection, the advice of the Economic Council of Canada given recently is both timely and sage:

> They (fiscal and monetary policies) might be more effec-
> tively employed with a view toward stabilizing larger economic
> fluctuations over longer time periods—that is, to moderating
> prolonged pressure against resources or reducing persistent
> economic slack.[11]

These comments may be interpreted to mean that appropriate and timely formulated long-range measures may be of more importance to economic growth than temporary expedients aimed at dealing with ad hoc problems, associated with short-term economic fluctuations.

In conclusion, then, there is enough instability in business life for Government not to resort to temporary expedients that would add to that instability. The objectives of sound fiscal policy presumably are equitability and effectiveness based on careful study. If these are the principles guiding Government, then it is difficult to justify makeshift arrangements and fiscal expedients, unsupported by adequate economic analysis.

---

[11] *Prices, Productivity and Employment, op. cit.,* pp. 165 and 166.

17

Findings

Based on the data presented in this study and subject to the qualifications explained, the findings may be summarized as follows:

1. *Trends in Advertising Expenditures.* Gross advertising expenditures amounted to approximately $821 million in 1966 and net advertising expenditures (i.e. after deducting advertising agency commissions) were about $766 million. Over the period 1946-1966, advertising expenditures have risen more rapidly than Gross National Product, 527 per cent as against 385 per cent. This trend has been reversed in the last five years (see Item 5 below).

2. *Projections of Advertising Expenditures.* Gross advertising expenditures may increase to between $1.1 billion and $1.2 billion in 1970 and between $1.7 and $1.9 billion by 1975, rising at least as rapidly as Gross National Product, and possibly at a moderately greater rate.

3. *Advertising Expenditures per Capita.* Advertising expenditures per capita amounted to about $41 in 1966, or about 11 cents per person per day. Some estimates suggest that at least two-thirds of all advertising expenditures made are "essential",

175

and that one-third represents "less essential" advertising. If all the "less essential" advertising in Canada could be eliminated, it may involve less than 4 cents per person per day. If such a cut-back were considered desirable, it could be achieved for example by removing all commercials from radio and television stations and by reducing newspaper advertising by one-third. This would force all private radio and television stations to close down, and the Canadian taxpayer would have to be prepared to pay one-quarter of the operating costs of the C.B.C., since this is the amount that is presently covered by revenues from advertising. Canadian newspapers would be unable to continue to give their readers the service they have been accustomed to.

4. *Advertising Expenditures and Revenues of Communication Media.* Advertising expenditures contribute 75 per cent to total revenues of newspapers and between 86 per cent and 95 per cent of total revenues of broadcasting stations.

5. *Advertising Expenditures and Gross National Product.* In 1966, advertising expenditures comprised 1.4 per cent of Gross National Product, estimated at about $57½ billion. Between 1961 and 1966, Gross National Product rose by 54 per cent and advertising expenditures by 37 per cent. The facts do not support the claim that advertising expenditures have been a strong contributing factor to inflationary pressures in the recent period, because Gross National Product, personal disposable income, consumer spending and personal savings have all risen more rapidly than advertising expenditures in Canada. (See Item 26 below.)

6. *National and Local Advertising Expenditures.* In 1966, national advertising expenditures made up 64½ per cent of total broadcast advertising and 31 per cent of newspaper advertising. Over the period 1961-1966, local advertising expenditures have risen more rapidly than national advertising expenditures: in the case of newspapers 34 per cent and 26 per cent respectively, while the opposite was the case for broadcasting, 67 per cent and 80 per cent respectively.

7. *Advertising Expenditures Going to Different Media.* Broadcast advertising is the most rapidly growing sector of advertising, though more recently a slow-down in the rate of growth of this type of advertising appears indicated. Broadcast advertising comprises currently about 23 per cent of the total (television 13 per cent and radio 10 per cent). The remainder is distributed as follows: newspapers, 37 per cent; periodicals, 13 per cent; all other printed media, 20 per cent; and other types of advertising, 7 per cent.

8. *Ratios of Advertising Expenditures to Sales.* In the majority of items, the ratio of advertising expenditures to sales value is between 1 and 2 per cent, with a considerable number of items showing ratios below 1 per cent and only three luxury or comfort items having ratios in excess of 10 per cent. The ratios are low for most essential items required for everyday living. Examples include: food and beverages, 1.6 per cent; motor cars, 1.4 per cent; bread and bakery products, 1.3 per cent; and children's clothing (factory), 0.2 per cent.

9. *Advertising and Economic Stability.* While evidence available is not fully conclusive, there are some indications that the pattern is changing and that in the postwar period advertising expenditures in Canada have been a positive factor in economic stability and a contributing element in economic growth. This is illustrated by the fact that advertising expenditures continued to increase during four periods of recession which Canada experienced since the end of World War II, as follows: 1948-1949 by 15 per cent; 1953-1954 by 10 per cent; 1957-1958 by 5 per cent; and 1960-1961 by 3 per cent. During three of the four recessions, Gross National Product continued to rise and only declined slightly during the 1953-1954 recession.

10. *Comparison with the United States.* The $41 that Canadians spent on advertising per capita in 1966 is equivalent to 49 per cent of the $84 per capita estimated to have been spent in the United States during the same year. In 1946, the ratio was 45 per cent. Reasons for the difference include: (a) differ-

ence in the size of the market, with the U.S. Gross National Product thirteen times that of Canada's; (b) national advertisers, the big spenders, are more important in the United States than in Canada; (c) American consumers are advertising-prone, more so than Canadian consumers; (d) spill-over effect of American advertising into Canada; (e) generally speaking, advertising costs per reader, listener or viewer, are higher in the United States than in Canada. Reasons why the gap in per capita advertising expenditures in Canada, as compared with the United States, have narrowed only slightly over the last twenty years include: (i) innovation lag; (ii) psychological lag; and (iii) expenditure lag.

11. *Advertising and Productivity.* Advertising can contribute to increasing productivity through expanding the scale of manufacturing operations by widening the market and through contributing to consumer acceptance of new or improved products which can be produced more economically than older products. But, in general, available cost data do not permit tracing of a clear causal relationship between decreased production costs and advertising.

12. *Advertising and Product Quality.* Industry studies undertaken in the United States show that advertising tended "decidedly" to improve quality and range of merchandise. Advertising has encouraged large-scale demand for specific products upon which often low prices depended and which in turn have been a stimulant to product improvement.

13. *Advertising and Product Differentiation.* Advertising, using mass media, has been a major factor in making possible product differentiation on a large scale in North America. Without denying that product differentiation, under certain circumstances, can go too far, proponents of advertising make the point that product differentiation has been proven successful because of the confidence built up among consumers in brand-name products. The reasoning supporting product differentiation runs as follows: Canada is a wealthy country and incomes of consumers

are rising. Consumers want a greater variety of goods and services to choose from. Who should say whether six varieties or twelve varieties of a particular product is the right number? There are three ways to deal with product differentiation: (a) let Government decide through controlling production and distribution; (b) let industry decide through reaching agreements amongst themselves; or (c) let market forces decide relying on competition and consumer acceptance as the determining factors. Public support in Canada appears to favour reliance on market forces rather than on government or industry controlling product differentiation.

14. *Advertising and the Product Innovator.* The product innovator or the product originator is the spark-plug of economic progress. He creates new products or brings improved products to the market. He makes an important contribution to the consumer in finding new ways to meet his wants and to provide him with an increasing number of choices as to how to spend his money and enjoy more his rising income and improved standard of living. The product originator will usually be the sponsor of a brand-name product and he will build up the acceptance of this product through extensive advertising. If successful, the brand-name product will bring the supplier increased profits and the consumer greater satisfaction. For a while, the product originator may have the market to himself, but as the market expands, other firms will enter it. These may be firms which have come forward with a similar product with a different brand-name. These brand-name product competitors will try to obtain their share of the expanding market by heavy advertising and other means. Sooner or later, however, a new type of competitor will enter the market—the product imitator.

15. *Advertising and the Product Imitator.* The product imitator brings to the market either the identical product or a product very similar to a brand-name product though it may not be identical in quality and performance to the brand-name product. The product imitator may spend little or no money on research and product development. He may incur modest or no

advertising expenditures in launching his products. He may give the impression that his product is as good as the one marketed under a brand-name. He may not give the same warranty or service as the brand-name product distributor. The non-brand-name or private-brand product will usually sell at a lower price than the corresponding brand-name product. Notwithstanding criticism by brand-name product suppliers, the product imitator may perform a socially useful service, mainly for three reasons: (a) by offering a low-priced product, he serves to uphold competition in advertising and other non-price forms; (b) he extends the range of products available to the consumer, and he may reach consumers in income brackets which the brand-name product supplier may not be able to reach; and (c) he spurs on the product originator to further product innovations because of the increased competition he is providing in the area of established products.

16. *Advertising and Mass Markets.* Advertising assists business firms in their efforts to obtain mass markets for their products. When such markets can be reached, the advantages of large-scale production and distribution will enable the entrepreneur to reap some of its benefits which may take the form of lower costs and higher profits. In many cases, the businessman may share the benefits from higher productivity with other factors of production, particularly labour and capital, and with the consumer, in terms of lower prices or the avoidance or lessening of price increases which may otherwise have become necessary.

17. *Advertising and Risk Minimization.* Advertising, if properly planned and soundly executed, can assist businessmen to minimize their risks because it gives them a measure of assurance of obtaining markets large enough to permit profitable operations. Thus, some businessmen look at advertising as an insurance against possible failure and as an essential requirement if they are to embark on large capital expenditures.

18. *Advertising and Capital Investment.* The interaction between advertising and investment has far-reaching implications

for economic and social progress, particularly in North America where both advertising and investment have reached higher levels than in any other continent in the world. But the contribution that advertising makes to facilitating an increasing volume of business investment is less clear-cut. Studies undertaken in this field in the United States have led to the following conclusion: "Advertising and aggressive selling as integral parts of the free competitive system have been a significant force in increasing the investment in productive facilities and in advancing the technology of production, two developments which have largely accounted for the fourfold increase of real national income per capita during the past 100 years."

19. *Advertising and the Consumer.* A principle of division of labour exists: advertising is undertaken by the businessman because he is able to do so in the most economic manner. By serving his own self-interest, he also serves the consumer. The consumer has the benefit in that advertising provides him with information about products, their availability, quality, price, etc., and increases his range of choice. The consumer does not pay for the advertising until he decides to purchase the commodity advertised.

20. *Self-Defence Mechanism of Consumer.* The consumer has developed a self-defence mechanism which enables him to resist some of the persuasive appeals addressed to him by advertisers. These include: (a) his determination not to spend more in *aggregate* than he is prepared to do; (b) he responds only to a few advertising appeals and he is not influenced by the majority of them; (c) he develops habits of thought of what he considers a "reasonable" price; (d) he develops certain associations with brand-name products and he may not repeat purchases if disappointed with the performance of the product; (e) he has in most instances a strong will to save and there is a point where the lures of advertising become ineffective; (f) he has a built-in aversion to "extravagant or misleading" advertising, and thus such advertising usually turns out to be ineffective in the long run; (g) he discounts a large measure of what is said in an ad-

vertisement, being well aware that the businessman is trying to sell him something; and (h) he has a certain loyalty to brand-name products and he may not take advertising that tries to persuade him to turn to another product very seriously.

21. *Public Control and Regulation of Advertising.* Advertising in Canada is controlled in certain areas both at the federal and at provincial levels. Examples of federal legislation affecting advertising include the Combines Investigation Act, the Food and Drug Act, the Opium and Narcotics Control Act, the Proprietary and Patent Medicine Act and the Broadcasting Act. Provincial legislation includes statutes that control the sale of alcoholic beverages.

22. *Consumer Education.* Consumer education involves providing the consumer with objective and disinterested information about the quality, serviceability and prices of goods and services, so as to enable him (a) to verify the claims made in business advertisements, and (b) to provide him with supplementary information which may assist him to make rational choices of alternatives open to him. Consumer education in Canada takes place in some schools and colleges, and through voluntary associations. Consumer education in Canada is not as yet well developed or widely spread, mainly because of the lack of initiative and the lack of funds. Since consumer education performs a socially useful function, it deserves encouragement.

23. *Advertising and Production Costs.* Advertising has in a number of instances contributed to the reduction of production costs by making it possible for management to achieve production economies in catering to a larger market, in part the result of advertising efforts. But in many other instances, advertising has added to production costs. Studies undertaken in the United States show that the answer to the question of advertising effects on production costs is indeterminate.

24. *Advertising and Distribution Costs.* Some critics claim that excessive advertising at the retail level is wasteful in that it

does not contribute to increasing total sales of particular commodities but rather affects the distribution among different
suppliers. The answer that has been given is that in fields in
which such intensive competition in advertising takes place,
the use of advertising, like the use of other forms of non-price
competition, has increased the costs of distribution, or has kept
them from being reduced. But the determining factor, from
society's point of view, is the decision the consumer makes. In
many instances the consumer has shown a willingness to pay
the costs involved in the vigorously advertised products, rather
than to turn to lower private-brand products. Available evidence
is inadequate to say whether in overall terms advertising has
contributed to raising distribution costs or reducing them. What
can be said is that the consumer, in exercising his prerogative
of choice, has been prepared to pay these costs.

~25. *Social Net Costs of Advertising.* The social net costs of
advertising may be measured in three ways: (a) the difference
in the gains in efficiency of production and distribution and the
additional costs of advertising involved; (b) the difference
between advertising expenditures and the costs of selling, employing techniques other than advertising; and (c) the difference
between total advertising expenditures and the subsidies made
available to communication media. No data of such subsidies are
available in Canada, but studies undertaken in the United States
suggest that a little more than one-half of advertising expenditures made were in effect subsidies to the print and broadcasting
media. In Canada, the proportion may be somewhat lower, possibly between one-third and two-fifths. If the consumer subsidy
to communication media were removed, for example, through
outright prohibition or a tax on advertising, this would lead
to severe cut-backs in services provided by the communication
media and would bring strong demands for government subsidies
to replace private subsidies.

26. *Advertising and Inflation.* During the period 1961-1966,
the following increases took place in Canada: personal disposable
income, 47 per cent, consumer expenditures, 43 per cent, personal

savings, 123 per cent, and advertising expenditures, 34 per cent. The figures do not support the contention that advertising expenditures have been a major factor contributing to inflationary pressures in the recent period, though more detailed studies are required to establish whether different developments have not in fact taken place in specific sectors and industries that are not apparent from aggregative figures.

27. *Advertising and Competition.* The consumer's greatest ally in getting the best possible service and the lowest price is the businessman who wants to obtain his patronage. And the process through which most businessmen endeavour to obtain what they consider a reasonable share of the consumer dollar is through competition. Advertising assists the businessman in selling his product. Thus it may serve the cause of competition. Competition in turn sharpens the search for latent consumer wants. Competition through advertising stimulates consumers to re-examine their consuming habits and presents them with an increasing range of choice. Competition has its ills and these may be magnified through advertising. Examples mentioned include: (a) forcible imposition on consumers, such as advertising to captive audiences; (b) limiting competition which may be based, among other means, on an understanding between the producers that nobody will offer to sell at a price below a certain acceptable minimum; and (c) in a situation where there are few sellers and where these virtually control all supplies among them—the economist speaks of an oligopoly situation—the sellers may decide to compete with each other by means of advertising, and although the consumers object to this they are unable to have recourse to unadvertised alternatives, since these do not exist.

28. *Advertising and Concentration.* Critics of advertising have been making the point increasingly in recent periods that large corporations may be using advertising as a means of reducing competition and supporting price maintenance, the result, in part, of growing concentration of industry. While enquiries in this area have been limited in Canada, a considerable amount of literature has been built up on the subject in the United States.

The main arguments of the anti-competitive effects of advertising have been summarized as follows: (a) the large company has the power of the large purse which enables it to spend substantial sums on advertising, particularly to implement product differentiation; (b) advertising thus creates a barrier to new firms entering industry; (c) the result is greater economic concentration; (d) because of their protected position, these firms charge monopolistic prices; and (e) high monopolistic prices in turn result in excessively larger profits. The defenders of advertising make three general points: (i) the claim that advertising is a significant factor in industrial concentration has not been proven; (ii) the suggestion that advertising contributes to raising prices and thus to inflation is not supported in overall terms by the postwar experience in the United States; and (iii) the point that industries with high advertising expenditures tend to earn considerably higher profit rates than industries making smaller advertising efforts appears to be not in accordance with the results obtained from research studies.

29. *Canadian Enquiry into the Economic Effects of Advertising.* An opportunity has arisen to undertake a Canadian enquiry into the economic effects of advertising in connection with the reference which the Canadian Government assigned to the Economic Council of Canada on July 26, 1966, in which the Council was asked to study and advise on the interests of consumers, particularly as they may be affected by combines, mergers, monopolies, restraint of trade, patents, trade marks, copyrights and registered industrial designs. In all these situations, advertising plays a role which could usefully be examined within the scope of the above-mentioned enquiry. Out of the deliberations and studies conducted by the Economic Council of Canada may evolve recommendations to the Government which could lead to a broader, more economic and less legalistic approach being made in Canada in the use of the provisions of the Combines Investigation Act.

30. *Tax on Advertising.* There are a number of ways of rationalizing a tax on advertising. One reason that has been

advanced recently is that a tax on advertising would contribute to reducing inflationary pressures in Canada. Objections to this proposal have been raised on the grounds that such a tax would inhibit business initiative and economic progress, and it would not contribute to lower prices or a lessening in aggregate demand. The main point appears to be that it is income rising in excess of the expanding capacity of the economy to produce goods and services that contributes to inflation of a "demand-pull" type, and not advertising. If this premise is accepted, then an income policy or higher income or other taxes are the answer, and not a tax on advertising.

The implications of the analysis, presented in this study and summarized in this section, are discussed in Chapter 18.

18

Implications

Lessons to be Learned From U.S. Experience

In the United States, voices are growing, both academic and public, asserting that excessive advertising contributes to market power, concentration of industry and reduction of competition. These claims are vigorously denied by industry leaders and the advertising profession, who are supported in part by some economists, few in number, though no less distinguished than their critical colleagues. The economists who support the case of the advertisers have in most instances the advantage that they are basing their judgment on research work and quantitative analysis undertaken in the field of the economic impact of advertising on the producer, the consumer, the mass communication media and society as a whole. This is not to say that research work is not being undertaken also by other economists who are, on the whole, critical of some of the alleged excesses of advertising, but it appears to be a fact that a good deal of the criticism is based on generalized analysis.

Looking at the controversy that presently occupies some of the finest minds in business, the professions and the Government, one cannot help being impressed by the complexity of the issues involved, and the difficulties encountered in delineating the problems involved and establishing causal relationships which can be quantified and verified.

To add to the complexity, the debate in the United States is taking place at two levels:

The first level is a discussion of the philosophical, moral, social and general economic issues involved, carried on in the trade press, the learned journals, and at conferences sponsored by industry associations and the professions, including lawyers, accountants, economists, political scientists, sociologists, etc.

This is an academic type of discussion that serves at times the useful purpose of clarifying some of the issues involved. These include such questions as: What is the morality of persuasion using powerful mass media? What price are Americans paying for the freedom of economic choice, presented to them in the greater number and more complex variety of goods and services offered to them through increasingly more sophisticated forms of advertising? Is the consumer able to protect himself or does he need protection? If so, at what point, and what kind of protection is desirable? Is there a point at which advertising becomes a threat to the public interest? If so, what is this point? Can it be established on general theoretical grounds? Are there certain principles that may assist in developing a national concensus on the issues involved?

The second level of discussion is of a more specific type. The Department of Justice in the United States has become increasingly concerned about the possibility that excessive advertising may play a similar role to that played by market concencentration. Mr. Donald F. Turner, the Assistant Attorney General in Charge of the Antitrust Division of the U.S. Department of Justice, has explained that his department takes "a dim view of excessive concentration precisely because it leads to monopoly results, and this is a major element of the rationale which underlies the laws prohibiting anticompetitive mergers. Current policies which tend to emphasize the role played by concentration may well need to be supplemented by those concerned directly with the adverse influences of advertising and other promotional efforts on competition."[1]

The attitude of the U.S. Government, in turn, is affecting business practices in the United States. Unending arguments ensue, with the courts finally deciding some of the issues involved in specific cases.

One level of discussion draws on another, but the encouraging feature of these discussions is that they have been moving in recent years away from the emotional debate to a more rational examination of the problems involved, based on results of quantitative assessment and research studies. Still, the evidence obtained and the results of the studies so far published are quite limited in scope and in many respects inconclusive, supporting neither the views advanced by the critics of advertising nor its defenders.

It is particularly telling that Professor Borden, in his monumental book, *The Economic Effects of Advertising*,[2] so far the most outstanding contribution in this field in the United States, and probably in the world, finds it necessary to say over and over again that evidence obtained from industry studies about the economic effects of advertising on specific aspects of economic activity are inconclusive or indeterminate.

What lessons can Canadians learn, in part from U.S. experience, and in part from their own? There are three lessons:

1. Policy solutions dealing with causes.

2. Research and measurement.

3. Consumer education and consumer affairs.

---

1 "Advertising and Competition", *op. cit.*, p. 6.
2 Richard D. Irwin, Inc., Homewood, Illinois, 1947.

Policy Solutions Dealing with Causes

The review of the literature and evidence obtainable, presented in this study, brings two main problems concerning advertising to the fore.

One is: Does advertising contribute to inflationary pressures by adding unnecessary costs to retail prices which fall particularly heavily on the shoulders of the consumers? This appears to be largely a cyclical problem, for much less is heard about high prices and the "burden" of excessive advertising in a period of slow growth or recession than is the case in a period of rapid economic growth and inflationary pressures.

The analysis presented in this study suggests that on the basis of evidence obtainable, no definite direct link can be established between higher advertising costs and rising retail prices in aggregate terms. But considerable evidence exists to support the suggestion that rising incomes, not fully matched by productivity increases, and such other factors as price increases transmitted from abroad, the effect of collective bargaining and indirect taxes, of business practices, etc.,[3] may contribute significantly to inflationary pressures. The effect on price increases is uneven and may be temporary, with some of the pressures easing as appropriate fiscal and monetary policies establish a "better" equilibrium between the forces of supply and demand.

If a main factor contributing to inflationary pressures is the level of income in relation to the physical capacity of the economy to produce goods and services, allowing for increases in production capabilities and in the labour force, then the policy action required would be one that deals with the cause of the inflationary pressures, say the high levels of income in relation to productive capacity, and not with advertising, which is a means of assisting in the proper functioning of the modern production and distribution system.

---

[3] *Prices, Productivity and Employment, op. cit.,* pp. 98 ff.

When incomes rise, it is not unnatural for businessmen to use additional advertising to get their share of the consumer dollar. If, on the other hand, incomes—that is, take-home pay or personal disposable income, as economists call it—rise at a lesser rate, for example because of a tax increase, then business-men would have less incentive to expand their advertising budgets knowing that the consumer market will not likely grow as much as it would have in the absence of the policy action taken by the Government.

Thus, a proper fiscal policy which encourages continuing economic expansion of an adequate rate over the longer term without too rapid rates of price increases, is likely to be a more effective means of keeping advertising expenditures in a reason-able relationship to total economic activity than would be a tax on advertising.

A tax on income in a period of inflation addresses itself to the cause of the problem. A tax on advertising would deal with the symptoms of the problem, but the end result would likely be increases in costs which would add to inflationary pressures rather than contribute to their reduction.

The situation is quite similar in the "big" debate as to whether advertising contributes significantly to concentration of industry and restraint of trade. Concentration of industry, combination, collusion, and all the other means that monopolists and oligo-polists may employ to safeguard their market power, are the basic cause of interference with competition in a free enterprise society. The solution to any problems in this area of undue market power—with the responsibility to prove their case resting on the shoulders of those who claim that such problems exist—would lie with the administration of combines legislation, and not with the primary control of advertising.[4]

Proper pursuit of anti-combines policy aims at dealing with the causes of the problem. Policies concerning the curtailment

---

4 See Professor Johnson's views on this subject, referred to in Section 2.

of advertising would deal only with the symptoms of the problem. Canadians can rely on the ingenuity of monopolists and oligopolists to find other means of achieving their objective if they cannot use advertising.

Thus, looking at advertising, both as a cyclical and a long-term factor affecting economic growth, if, under certain circumstances it may bring adverse effects to the economy, the way to deal with it is to apply policy action to the basic causes that contribute to the problem. It may require raising income tax in periods of inflation. It may require strengthening and tightening of combines policy in periods when competition is willfully reduced.

The national interest can best be served if government measures go to the root of the problem rather than use expedients to knock over a straw man.

Research and Measurement

It has been stated earlier that after twenty years of research and statistical investigations of many types, mainly carried on in the United States, there is still insufficient quantitative information and professional assessment available to formulate an objective judgment on the relative value or disutility of such an important service as advertising.

The United States, with its wealth of professional and financial resources, can afford research to proceed along many unrelated lines, but Canada with her more limited resources cannot. Even in the United States, however, views differ as to how much effort should be devoted to research. The leaders of industry say not enough is being done. One of the strong supporters of doing more research in the communication area is J. Emmet Judge, the Vice President of Marketing Research of Westinghouse Electric Corporation in the United States. To quote: "We think that in all areas of advertising we ought to put into research between 2 and 3 per cent of our total communications investment. I would put money into research even if it meant reducing the amount of exposure."[5]

While a strong case can be made for doing more research in the advertising field in Canada also, and in fact such a case has been made on a number of occasions throughout this study, such research cannot in all respects follow the American pattern.

What would be involved in putting research dealing with the economic implications of advertising on a proper footing in Canada, considering the limited resources available? There are six aspects to this question:

First, an outline would be required of the research program, broad enough to cover the interest of all sectors of the economy, industry, labour, consumer, communication media, advertising profession and government. But at the same time, the program would, in the first stage, have to be limited in order to be practical of application, and realizable over, say, the next five years.

Second, a system of priorities would have to be established so that the most urgent studies could be undertaken first.

Third, administrative machinery and advisory committees would have to be set up representing the professions and the various interest groups, as well as public bodies.

Fourth, adequate funds would have to be provided to ensure the continuity of the research program, with such funds coming from all participating sectors, including government, so that the underwriting of the program of research carried with it not only an expression of interest, but also a willingness to support this interest in a tangible manner. The funds would have to be adequate to finance not only the research but also the publication of the results obtained.

Fifth, the independence and objectivity of such research efforts would have to be assured, and this presumably could be

---

5 "Ad Mood Changes", by J. Emmet Judge, *New York Herald-Tribune*, August 17, 1965.

done through careful selection of the research director in charge of the program, the integrity of the professional staff engaged in the research and the high calibre of the members of the advisory committees that would guide the development of the research program.

Sixth, industry, government and professional cooperation would be essential to the success of such a research program to ensure that the work done produced the best possible results in the area of the effects of advertising on industrial and consumer behaviour, and on social and national welfare in general.

To implement the six requirements, as set out above, involves:

1. The collection of adequate statistics obtained on a continuing and comparable basis, relating to advertising and its economic effects. These could be most appropriately obtained by making use of the facilities of the Dominion Bureau of Statistics.

2. The undertaking of a comprehensive research program would require the establishment of an institute of advertising research. Such an institute would differ somewhat from the Canadian Advertising Research Foundation, as it presently exists, in two respects. It would be more broadly based, representing all major interested sectors in the economy. And it would have a more comprehensive research function to fulfil, based on a system of priorities which serve the best national interest. This is not to say that the functions and organization of the Canadian Advertising Research Foundation could not be altered to meet all the requirements as set out above.[6]

---

6 The Advertising Research Foundation in the United States, first established in 1936 and broadened out considerably in 1951, performs somewhat more extended functions than its Canadian counterpart. The objectives of the American Foundation include: "1. To further, through the fostering of research, scientific practices in advertising and marketing. 2. To make consultation and advisory facilities available to the industry. 3. To establish research standards, criteria, and reporting methods. 4. To offer consultative and professional guidance in the conduct of research studies of general interest to regular members in cooperation with interested groups. 5. To review and
(Footnote continued on next page)

This could be done if such a reorganization met the wishes of all concerned. As important as the development of such a research program appears to be, it may be wise counsel to make haste slowly in developing first a research program before establishing an organization.

There exists an alternative to establishing a separate research body concerned with advertising research in Canada. This would be the establishment of an advertising research fund, administered by one of the government departments, possibly the Department of Industry,[7] or a Department of Consumer Affairs, should such a department be established at some future date.[8] The government department would then operate the research fund along similar lines as, for example, is now the case with

appraise published research. 6. To analyze and evaluate existing research methods and techniques and to define their proper applications and limits of usefulness. 7. To help develop new research techniques. 8. To collect and disseminate advertising and marketing research data and information." (For further details, see "The Advertising Research Foundation: Why, How, and for Whom?", by Alcuin W. Lehman, in *Marketing Research, op. cit.*, p. 210.)

7 For the studies to be effective, they would have to be undertaken on an industry and commodity basis. The Department of Industry, with its knowledge and contacts with industry, could make a constructive contribution to the development of such a research program. As a useful by-product, research into the economic effects of advertising and promotion would bring to the fore information on productivity changes in industry and some of the factors contributing to it—a subject of particular interest to the Department of Industry in the Federal Government.

8 The Institute of Canadian Advertising recommended: "Consumer education would deal with the process of communicating information on family and personal budgeting, household economics, and general product information. This effort should be supplemented by continuing policy consideration of problems affecting the welfare of the consumer. This kind of consideration could be entrusted to an Advisory Council on Consumer Affairs which, on the basis of studies and the general knowledge of the problems involved, could advise government, the legislature and the public on the nature of these issues and the policy solutions that might be considered. . . . Such an Advisory Council on Consumer Affairs could be a newly-established body. Or, its functions could be performed by the Economic Council of Canada, as presently constituted, but with its terms of reference expanded to cover consumer affairs." (See *Proceedings* of the Special Joint Committee of the Senate and House of Commons on Consumer Credit (Prices), December 13, 1966, pp. 2012 and 2013.)

Central Mortgage and Housing Corporation administering research funds on housing and urban development under Part V
of the National Housing Act, 1954.

An outline of possible subjects for research in the field of
advertising and its economic impact is included in the Appendix.

Consumer Education
and Consumer Affairs

How can consumer education be strengthened in Canada? Do
people really want to be told how to shop more effectively? How
many housewives will in fact go to the trouble of obtaining independently compiled information on consumer goods, their
quality and prices, even if such information were available just
for the asking by writing to either a consumer organization or a
government department?

Again the views differ on the subject. Consumer, labour, and
other citizen groups say it is essential to make such information
available to consumers. Some business groups say: Let us encourage consumer education. If it helps, fine; if not, let us not
waste time or money!

But the situation is not as simple as that. Consumer education
is adult education. Is this a federal or a provincial responsibility?
Is this an effort that industry should support or would such
support be suspect? Is voluntary effort enough?

Or is there need for a three-pronged approach: consumer,
industry and government? Or alternatively, should government
take a more direct hand in consumer education than has been
considered either desirable or necessary up to the present time?
Has the time come to establish a new Government Department
of Consumer Affairs, or to extend the responsibilities of an existing department to look after the interest of consumers on a
continuing basis? There are a number of departments in the
Federal Government that look after industry, trade and labour,

but which department of the Federal Government is charged with this specific task of looking after the interest of the consumer?

Would it be practical to have the Department of Justice, which administers the Combines Investigation Act, to become the prime department responsible for protecting the interest of the consumer by pursuing enquiries entrusted to it under the Act? Or, is the question of protecting the consumer interest a broader matter of fiscal and monetary policies administered by the Department of Finance, in cooperation with the Bank of Canada?

Or has the consumer become such an important fact of Canadian political life to justify the appointment of an economic advisor to the Prime Minister concerned with consumer affairs? Or has the time come for the Canadian Government to appoint a broadly based Advisory Committee on Consumer Affairs to advise the Government on problems that confront the consumer?[9]

Or is it possible that the Special Joint Senate-House of Commons Committee on Consumer Credit (Prices) will have concluded after completing its hearings that the problems concerning the Canadian consumer are not just a matter of credit and rising prices considered in the temporary context of a phase in the business cycle, but as a continuing problem that requires the attention of a Continuing Special Joint Senate-House of Commons Committee on Consumer Affairs?

These are the kinds of questions that may occupy decision makers in the legislature, government, industry, labour and consumer groups.

Conclusion

The main implications presented in this study can be re-stated in conclusion as follows:

---

[9] The United States has already given a lead in this field, with the appointment of the Special Assistant to the President, concerned with Consumer Affairs, and the establishment of the President's Committee on Consumer Interests.

There may be need to:

1. Formulate economic policy to deal with causes of problems rather than symptoms. To illustrate: If inflation over the short term is largely the result of income levels being raised at a more rapid rate than the capacity of the economy to produce goods and services, then the most appropriate way of dealing with the situation is to attack the causes of the problem through an incomes policy or fiscal policy, and not through an attack on the symptoms of the problem like a tax on advertising.

2. Take a broader approach to economic growth policy. For example, if over the longer term one of the main problems contributing to an inadequate rate of economic growth is restraint of trade exercised by some large corporations with the help of excessive advertising, then the answer is to use the provisions of the Combines Investigation Act to deal with collusion, price maintenance and reduction of competition, rather than with the means employed to commit unlawful acts—if these can be proven.

3. Undertake the collection of adequate and comparable statistics on advertising and its economic effects on a continuing basis, presumably by the Dominion Bureau of Statistics.

4. Provide for a comprehensive and continuing research and study program in the field of advertising and its economic effects, including the establishment of a new Institute of Advertising Research, or alternatively, the establishment of an Advertising Research Fund, administered by a government department, either the Department of Industry or a new Department of Consumer Affairs, if such a department were established.

5. Encourage the development of a comprehensive program of consumer education and protection, as well as of general public enlightenment. By publishing the results of research studies as well as pertinent statistics on a continuing basis, together with reports issued as a result of enquiries under the Combines Investigation Act, the public would be apprised of what was going on, thus assisting in the crystallization of views

as to the various claims that are made about the merits and demerits of advertising.

6. Consider placing consumer interests as a matter of continuing concern of Parliament and of Government. The former could be achieved by establishing a Continuing Special Joint Senate-House of Commons Committee on Consumer Affairs, taking the place of the present Special Joint Senate-House of Commons Committee on Consumer Credit (Prices). The latter could be achieved by appointing an economic advisor to the Prime Minister on consumer affairs and/or establishing an Advisory Committee on Consumer Affairs reporting to the Government of Canada through the Privy Council.

Appendix

This appendix lists some of the areas of research and measurement in the field of advertising and its impact on the economy that have been mentioned throughout this study. Page numbers of the references in this study are shown in brackets.

1. Basic evidence and assessment is needed to facilitate an examination of the claim that "excessive" advertising is an aid to monopolistic and oligopolistic business practices which in turn have contributed to interfering with the principles of the "best" obtainable resource allocation, and with competition in Canada. (See page 18.)

2. Information is needed to establish whether or not advertising contributes to rising prices at the factory level, the wholesale level, the retail level and the general price level, and whether it adds to inflationary pressures in aggregate terms. (See pages 26 and 136ff.)

3. Data are needed either to support or to refute the claim that industries with intensive advertising have such a degree of market power that they increase prices significantly in a period of inflation, undeterred by market forces. (See page 27.)

201

4. Quantitative evidence would be helpful to demonstrate whether firms making large advertising expenditures do in fact obtain much higher profit ratios on capital investment than firms making smaller advertising efforts. (See page 27.)

5. Research is needed to delineate the different impact that advertising may have on economic activity in periods of cyclical change and on economic growth over the longer term. (See page 29.)

6. Continuing annual statistics on a comparable basis are required covering *all* advertising expenditures made in Canada, distinguishing between gross and net advertising expenditures by type of industry, by type of commodity, and by type of communication media, replacing the incomplete data now being collected. Also, the publication of the data could usefully be speeded up, for at present it takes between two and three years after the event for published data to become available. (See pages 32 ff.)

7. Measurement is required of national and local advertising. Specific areas needing quantification are advertising allowances made available by national firms to regional or local distributors. (See pages 41 ff.)

8. Surveys of the ratios of advertising expenditures to sales are required on a continuing basis, providing data for different industries, wholesale and retail sectors and service establishments. The last such survey was undertaken by the Dominion Bureau of Statistics in 1954. (See page 45.)

9. Measurement and assessment of the spill-over effect of American advertising into Canada would be helpful. (See page 48.)

10. Research work is needed with respect to the cyclical behaviour of advertising expenditures and economic activity and including a comparison of Canadian experience with that of the United States and other countries. (See pages 58 ff.)

11. Surveys are needed to facilitate the assessment of the effectiveness of advertising through the use of various media and on various groups of consumers, covering not only the economic aspects, but also social, psychological and human factors involved. (See page 72.)

12. Additional information and analysis is required on the subject of the effect of advertising on product quality and product differentiation, and the benefits such developments bring to the consumer. (See pages 80 ff.)

13. More study is needed of the economic and social function of the product originator and the product imitator, and the role of advertising in this area. (See pages 94 ff.)

14. Research is required to establish whether a causal relationship exists between advertising and capital investment, and the extent of it, if it does exist, under different economic circumstances, in different industries, among different firms, and in different phases of the business cycle, and over the longer term. (See pages 98 ff.)

15. More information is required to assess consumer attitudes and reactions to different types of advertising, as well as the effect of advertising on consumer purchases distinguishing between different commodities, for different income classes, and over time, rather than as at a point of time. (See page 111.)

16. Enquiry would be helpful into how effective the self-defence mechanism, developed by consumers, is in response to stepped-up advertising. (See pages 112 and 113.)

17. Statistics of advertising expenditures, specifically directed at the consumer (as distinct from industry, governments and institutions), is required, on a commodity basis, with the data thus obtained comparable to the grouping of consumer expenditure items, as contained in the National Accounts. (See page 115.)

18. Thorough examination of production and distribution costs is needed, and the manner and extent to which they are affected by rising advertising expenditures. (See pages 119 ff.)

19. Research is needed to establish the social *net* costs of advertising, and particularly the subsidy effect of advertising expenditures on newspapers, broadcasting stations and other communication media. (See pages 130 ff.)

20. Assessment is required of what the economic impact of a tax on advertising may be in terms of cost to producers and distributors, in terms of prices to consumers, and in terms of the effect on the rate of economic growth—a matter of concern to the nation as a whole. (See pages 159 ff.)

Index